DEFENDING YOUNG OFFENDER CASES

1997

This edition prepared by:
Sheena Scott

Founding authors:
Mavin Wong
and
Brian Weagant

CARSWELL
Thomson Professional Publishing

Canadian Cataloguing in Publication Data

Wong, Mavin
    Defending young offender cases 1997

(Canada practice guide. Criminal)
Rev. ed.
Includes bibliographical references and index.
ISBN 0-459-55512-X

1. Juvenile justice, Administration of – Canada.
2. Juvenile courts – Canada. 3. Defense (Criminal procedure) – Canada. I. Weagant, Brian. II. Scott, Sheena.
III. Title. IV. Series.

KE9448.W65 1997   345.71'08   C97-930691-4
KF9779.W65 1997

CARSWELL
Thomson Professional Publishing

One Corporate Plaza, 2075 Kennedy Road, Scarborough, Ontario M1T 3V4
Customer Service:
Toronto 1-416-609-3800
Elsewhere in Canada/U.S. 1-800-387-5164
Fax 1-416-298-5094

Summary Table of Contents

For a detailed Table of Contents, see page v.

Table of Contents

Chapter 5
PREPARATION FOR TRIAL

Chapter 6
THE TRIAL

Chapter 7
MEDICAL AND PSYCHOLOGICAL REPORTS/
FITNESS AND SANITY

Chapter 8
TRANSFER APPLICATIONS

Chapter 9
DISPOSITIONS OF THE COURT

Chapter 10
REVIEW OF DISPOSITIONS

Chapter 11
RECORDS

Chapter 12
MISCELLANEOUS

Introduction

The representation of young persons who are being prosecuted under the *Young Offenders Act* necessitates a distinctive approach to traditional criminal practice. The juvenile justice legislation is more than just a procedural code which sets out a unique sentencing scheme and circumscribes the traditional law of admission of confessions. It is legislation which tries to distinguish between adults and young persons by bringing special policies to bear at all stages of prosecution.

In addition to the traditional considerations which inform the process in adult matters, there are additional policies enshrined in section 3 of the *Young Offenders Act* which must be applied by a court in the case of young persons.

Of particular importance to defence counsel are the following:

○ A multi-disciplinary approach to crime prevention is favoured: section 3(1)(*a*);
○ Bearing responsibility is not synonymous with suffering adult-like accountability: section (3)(1)(*a*.1);
○ The antecedents to the criminal behaviour are relevant, as reasonable measures should be taken by society to prevent criminal behaviour in teens: section (3)(1)(*b*);
○ Rehabilitation through addressing the needs of the youth is the best means of achieving the protection of society: section 3(1)(*c*.1);
○ Young persons are entitled to the least possible interference with freedom that is consistent with protection of society: section (3)(1)(*f*);
○ Young persons should only be removed from their families when measures cannot be taken which would provide for continuing parenting: section (3)(1)(*h*).

What follows is a practical guide to help the first-time practitioner or the criminal lawyer who is not at home in youth court. This guide deals only with those aspects of the justice process which are unique to young persons under the *Young Offenders Act*.

References in the text to the Young Offenders Act are abbreviated as Y.O.A.

1

THE PHONE CALL FROM THE POLICE STATION

1.1 GENERAL

The initial telephone call from a young person at the police station, or from a distraught parent, may be the lawyer's first contact with the client and your client's first encounter with the police. It is crucial, therefore, to remember the following:

- Explain the procedure in a language appropriate to the age and understanding of your client.

- Do not assume anything about your client's knowledge of the process even if your client has been arrested before.

1.2 HOW TO STRUCTURE THE CALL

1.2.1 NOTES

- Make notes of the entire conversation, including notes concerning the physical surroundings as described by your client.

1.2.2 PRIVACY

- Ensure that your client is speaking to you in private.

  - Ask if your client is in a room by him or herself and if the door is shut.

  - If your client is not alone, ask to speak to the person present.

- If the person is a police officer, ask the officer to let your client speak to you in private. However, first you may want to ascertain from the officer:

  - the charges;

  - the time of arrest;

  - if your client has given a statement;

  - if the officer intends to take a statement;

  - if the parents have been notified;

  - if any decision has been made regarding the release or detention of the client;

  - the name of the officer, badge number and police division.

1.2.3 OBTAINING CLIENT INFORMATION

- Once privacy is certain, obtain the following information from your client:

  - name, age and birthdate;

  - charges;

  - length of time in detention;

  - parents.

    - Does he or she live with his or her parents?

    - Are his or her parents at the police station?

    - Does he or she want his or her parents or another adult to come to the police station?

- If he or she wants his or her parents, *make sure that you advise the officer to wait for the parents/ adult.*

- Let your client know that under the *Young Offenders Act*, notice to a parent or guardian is mandatory. If your client knows parents must and will be notified of the charge, he or she may want you to contact them before the police do so.

1.2.4 OBTAINING INFORMATION ABOUT EVENTS AT THE STATION

- Get the following information from your client:

  - Physical health — any injuries or complaints?

  - Has he or she given a "statement" within the meaning of the *Young Offenders Act? Most youths will have an inaccurate view of what a statement is.*

    - Explain to your client that a statement could be any comment or answer made, usually to the police, though a statement can also be made to a parent or other person.

1.2.5 ADVICE TO GIVE

- Advise your client that he or she is not obliged to answer any questions asked by the police except those questions which relate to his or her full and proper name and age.

- Tell your client that you strongly advise not answering any other questions.

- Advise your client that police may show him or her statements made by the co-accused which blame him or her for the alleged offence. Without giving your client a lesson on the admissibility of co-accused's statements, tell your client not to be swayed into telling "his or her side of the story". (Counsel should see *R. v. B. (K.G.)*, [1993] 1 S.C.R. 740, 19 C.R. (4th) 1, 79 C.C.C. (3d) 257.)

○ Advise your client not to sign or initial anything except a release document (for example, a promise to appear, or undertaking) but add that this should be read carefully first. Emphasize that this is the only document that should be signed.

○ Advise your client not to go with the police to either retrieve certain property or show the police where other offences may have been committed. Advise that there is no obligation to go with the police and that the invitation should be refused. *Police may attempt to have your client incriminate him or herself further by employing one of these methods.*

○ Advise your client not to be persuaded into giving or signing a statement because the police say things like "it is better for you if you co-operate" or "if you don't tell us about these incidents, we will charge you with more".

○ Advise your client that the police *may* permit necessary phone calls, but *must* permit calls to you, or put your call through.

○ Seek instruction from your client to advise the police that he or she will not be giving a statement.

○ Pass this information along to the police officer, and record the officer's name and the time you hang up the phone.

2

THE FIRST IN PERSON CONTACT: INTERIM RELEASE

2.1 PROVISIONS FOR RELEASE

Other than a situation where you get a call from the police station, the form of release of a young person may dictate the initial contact.

- As with adult offenders, young persons may be released after arrest in several ways:

  - Summons to Attend (*Form 6*, section 509 *Criminal Code*).

  - On an Appearance Notice (*Form 9*) or Promise to Appear (*Form 10*), when the young person is being released from the scene of the arrest or the police station.

  - On a Recognizance before the officer-in-charge (*Form 11*) or an Undertaking given to a Justice of the Peace (*Form 12*) when the young person is released from the police station on conditions.

  - On an Undertaking given to a judge or justice (*Form 12*) or a Recognizance with or without sureties, when released from a court.

- Unlike adults, young persons are susceptible to release under a unique provision of the *Young Offenders Act* wherein a responsible person in the community undertakes to the court to enter into an undertaking of supervision. Release takes place as follows:

  - The young person is released to a responsible adult on a *Form 2* of the *Young Offenders Act* under section 7.1.

○ The responsible person also enters into an undertaking in *Form 1* of the *Young Offenders Act.*

2.2 BAIL HEARINGS

Generally, the Part XVI sections of the *Criminal Code* relating to judicial interim release orders apply to young offenders. Issues such as whether or not the onus to show cause is on the Crown or on the defence do not change because it is a young offender's proceeding. (Counsel are advised to see *Carswell's Practice Guide: Bail by Burrows*, for guidance on how to conduct a bail hearing generally.)

The strategy and the way you conduct the hearing, however, may be different.

○ While in all cases you must persuade the court that the plan of release you propose satisfies both the primary and secondary grounds, in the case of young persons, justices or judges may also be concerned about the following issues:

○ Questions about the ability of the proposed surety to supervise your client will be very important. *Unlike adult show cause hearings, it may not be sufficient on the issue of release to simply have a judge order a recognizance and worry later about finding someone to sign the bail.*

○ The nature of any proposed supervision.

○ The likelihood that your client will have an opportunity to reoffend if not properly supervised.

○ Be prepared to persuade the court that there is a workable plan in the community which will offer the court assurance that your client will return to court and will not reoffend. *Your ability to persuade the court of this will determine, in many cases, your client's ability to obtain bail.*

○ Explore the following areas and consider directing questions to these areas during a show cause hearing:

○ If your client's parents work outside the home, what are their hours of work?

○ If the parents have hours which coincide neatly with when your client leaves and returns home from school, then emphasize the parents' ability to supervise the child.

○ If the parents have work hours which result in gaps in the parents' ability to personally supervise your client, question the family further about other relatives or responsible neighbours who would be able to supervise during the problem times.

○ If your client has a special relationship with his or her siblings and responds well to their instruction, emphasize this added supervision.

○ Determine how your client perceives his or her family and their relationship. If your client indicates that they have a good, healthy and honest relationship, emphasize this. *Confirm this with the parents before asking the questions in open court.*

○ If your client's relationship with his or her family is not positive, but the parents are still prepared to act as a surety and have your client reside at home, speak to the parents before court about their obligation to call police and revoke the bail, if the child fails to comply with conditions of release. *Even where the child-parent relationship is arguably under some stress, a parent who appears to be fully informed about his or her obligations as a surety and is prepared to strictly enforce the court's rules may be a suitable surety.*

○ Always ask your client and the proposed surety if they have discussed the offence with each other. While your client cannot be asked at the show cause hearing whether or not he or she committed the offence, any other person called as a witness can be questioned about what your client has said. *An admission by your client that he or she "did it", particularly if the allegations are serious, can be very damaging to his or her chances for release.*

o Ask the parents if they have ever acted as sureties before for your client and if they did, ask how the child
responded and whether there were any difficulties.

o Emphasize past compliance in your questions and argument.

o If there has been non-compliance in the past, determine
whether the parent may have taken some positive steps
such as contacting police and reporting the behaviour.
If so, bring this out in questioning the parents.

o If the parents admit that they had little control over the
child in the past, or the youth record reveals a series of
non-compliance offences, it may be wise to avoid this
area of questioning.

o Ask the parents if there are any specific conditions which
they wish to have imposed by the court. *Note, this question can be dangerous; it may be an invitation for a concerned and, perhaps, over zealous parent to begin a
checklist of conditions which may not be appropriate for
the nature of the offence or the criminal history of your
client. Remember, you are acting on behalf of the young
person, and not on behalf of the parent.*

o If the charge is very serious or other factors dictate that
release is questionable, exploring the above area with
a witness who is concerned and responsible may im-
press a court and may result in the release of your client.

o If the child is going to attend a day program or school,
determine where it is located and how long does it take
to travel from the school to home. *This may be an important question if a strict curfew is being considered.*

o If the child is to reside in a group home, determine if the
school is located within the facility.

o If the evidence shows that your client has not been attending school regularly, explore the possibility of any

learning disabilities which may help explain your client's frustration with school and which may discourage regular attendance.

○ Remember to raise the principles underlying the *Act* and contained in section 3, in arguing for release (see section 9.3.1 below). In spite of the fact that the law regarding judicial interim release applies in the case of young persons, the principle of least possible interference with freedom *also* applies. Do not ignore this principle when pleading for a young person's release.

2.3 NON-TRADITIONAL FAMILY SITUATIONS: THE INVOLVEMENT OF CHILD WELFARE AGENCIES

One of the realities of acting for young offenders is that a large percentage of your clients live or are under the supervision and care of child care agencies.

○ The extent of child welfare agencies' involvement will vary from case to case. In Ontario, a young person may be involved with the Children's Aid Society in any of the following ways*:

○ The young person may be receiving services under some sort of 'voluntary care agreement'. This means that there is no court order binding the arrangement, but the parents, Children's Aid and the young person have entered into a contract which temporarily transfers parenting power to the Children's Aid.

○ Limitations on the scope of Children's Aid's degree of control will be set out in the agreement. For example,

---

* The Act governing child welfare agencies in Ontario is the *Child and Family Services Act*, R.S.O. 1990, c. C11. The child welfare acts in other provinces are as follows: *Child Welfare Act*, R.S.A. 1984, c. C-8.1; *Family and Child Services Act*, R.S.B.C. 1980, c. 11; *Child and Family Services Act*, R.S.M. 1985-86, c. 8; *Family Services Act*, S.N.B. 1980, c. F-22; *Child Welfare Act*, R.S.N. 1990, c. C-12; *Child Welfare Act*, R.S.N.W.T. 1988, c. C-6; *Child and Family Services Act*, S.N.S. 1990, c. 5; *Family and Child Services Act*, R.S.P.E.I. 1988, c. F-2; *Youth Protection Act*, R.S.Q., c. P-34.1; *Child and Family Services Act*, S.S. 1989-90, c. C-7.2; *Children's Act*, R.S.Y. 1987, c. 25.

Children's Aid may be entitled to make medical decisions where the parents' consent would otherwise be required by law.

○ These agreements can be cancelled at the behest of the young person or the parents, but statute may provide a grace period within which the Children's Aid may have the opportunity to consider the commencement of protection proceedings before the agreement is ended.

○ Be aware of this type of child welfare status when the question of a surety is explored with your client.

○ The young person and his family may be under an order referred to as a "supervision" order. This means that custody and care is retained by the family unit but the Children's Aid holds a supervisory power over the arrangement.

○ This is the least intrusive form of court order which follows a family court finding that a young person is in need of protection at the time of apprehension by Children's Aid or at the time of its initial involvement.

○ The young person may be a ward of the Children's Aid Society. Unless specific power is reserved to the parents, this form of court order effectively substitutes the Society as parent. *Note, in this case, the Society becomes the "parent", for purposes of "Notice to Parent" and surety considerations.*

○ The Society wardship is generally limited by provincial child welfare legislation to particular length of time.

○ The young person may be a ward of the Crown. This means that parental rights and obligations, unless specifically reserved by court order (such as access), are severed in favour of Children's Aid parenting. The Society remains the parent until the young person is of a specified age, usually 18 years.

○ Note that the age at which a young person can be taken into care varies across the provinces. The age in Ontario is 16. Voluntary services and services to youth already in care are available beyond the age of 16. Familiarity with provincial child welfare laws will assist you in advising your client.

○ Note, some provincial legislation, notably Ontario's, allows for the Children's Aid to apply for discharge of a ward at the age of 16. *Effectively, youths discharged at this age have no 'parent' to look to — they are emancipated. Bail release programs will obviously figure more largely in the judicial interim release considerations for these young persons.*

2.3.1 EFFECT ON BAIL APPLICATIONS

○ In many situations, the presence of the child care agency may be helpful in obtaining a release for your client. Where the agency is supportive of the child and is offering a residential placement or a treatment plan, many Crown attorneys may be prepared to consent to the young person's release.

○ If a Crown does not consent to the release, a judge may release the child to the agency with appropriate conditions.

○ Be prepared for those situations where an agency worker comes to court, is adamant that the agency cannot or will not provide a placement for the youth and refuses to offer any helpful suggestions other than that the client should be held in detention. *This situation can be quite common. The youth may have consistently run away from previous placements, or has displayed aggressive, inappropriate or challenging behaviour. The social worker may see the criminal charge as being a way of 'dumping' an otherwise difficult situation.*

○ You must, in this situation, navigate around various parties and still try to obtain a release for the youth. *A youth ought not to be detained simply because the Children's Aid Society refuses to place him or her.* You may be able to ask for an order placing the youth in the care of a Childrens' Aid Society whether or not the society is in agreement. Ensure your client's agreement to such a request.

o Keep in mind that the Society is the young person's parent by law. Should the child be released from the court, the agency is *obligated* to find a placement. Remind the parties that the agency, while having some legitimate concerns over their ability to safely keep and maintain a child, should not be able to use the criminal courts and detention as a solution to their problems. *You may be frustrated by Crown attorneys, child care workers, and many times, judges, who do not understand the conflicting interests.*

2.4 TRANSFER APPLICATIONS: EFFECT OF CONDUCT ON BAIL HEARING

o Where your client is 16 or 17 and charged with certain serious offences, the matter will be dealt with in adult court unless you apply to youth court to transfer the matter down to youth court ("transfer down" hearing).

o Where there is no automatic transfer and the charge is likely to result in a transfer application, determine as early as possible whether the Crown intends to proceed in this way.

o Where a transfer hearing is upcoming, use the bail hearing to thoroughly cross-examine the officer or detective who prepared the Crown's synopsis of the case. *This is a free practice run at the officer-in-charge who will certainly be called at the transfer hearing to state the allegations.*

o See Chapter 8 herein.

2.5 RELEASE TO A RESPONSIBLE PERSON — SECTION 7.1

The *Young Offenders Act* has always recognized the important role of parents. In section 1 of the Act, a ''parent'' is defined as any person who is under a legal duty to provide for the young person, or who has by law or in fact the custody or control of the young person. Under the Declaration of Principles, in subsections 3(*c*), (*f*) and most particularly (*h*), the relationship between parents and their children is tremendously important.

○ The special nature of the relationship of a child with his or her parent or guardian is recognized in the provisions of section 7.1 of the *Young Offenders Act*. Under this section, a young person who would otherwise be detained in custody, may be released into the care of a responsible person.

○ The responsible person must not only be willing and able to take care of and exercise control over the young person, but must also be willing to sign an undertaking in writing to the court.

○ The responsible person must undertake in writing to take care of and be responsible for the attendance of the young person in court when required and ensure that the child complies with any conditions the youth court imposes.

○ The young person must also sign an undertaking agreeing to the arrangement.

  ○ This section is most helpful where your client is already before the court on a number of previous releases or is charged with a very serious offence and has a terrible youth record. Where a parent or other adult comes forward and testifies that he or she is prepared to risk the possibility of being charged with an offence, it can be very persuasive to a justice or judge to give the child one more chance.

  ○ Remember to argue that the Declaration of Principles in section 3 (see section 9.3.1 below) mandates the court to explore all options for release before a detention order is made.

○ Section 7.2 states that any person who wilfully fails to comply with the conditions imposed in the undertaking or with section 7, is guilty of an offence punishable on summary conviction.

   ○ It should be noted that the "responsible person" can apply for relief of his or her duties and obligations by applying in writing to the youth court.

2.6 BAIL REVIEWS — SECTION 8

○ Become familiar with section 8 of the *Young Offenders Act.* In some jurisdictions and in the practice of some lawyers, section 8 is the most under-utilized and misunderstood provision of the *Act.*

   ○ Section 8 provides that where an order is made before a justice of the peace detaining or releasing your client, an application may be made for a review of the disposition upon two clear days' written notice being served on the opposing party.

   ○ See *Appendix B, Form 3* for a sample of the Form of Notice required for this purpose.

○ Section 8(2) says that the youth court shall hear the matter as an original application. This means a bail hearing *de novo.*

   ○ Note, the effect of this section is that unlike bail review applications for adult offenders, where a young person is detained or released by a justice of the peace, a bail review can be heard before a youth court judge without the requirement of the transcript, a copy of the information, or affidavits being filed.

   ○ Written notice may be waived by the prosecutor or by the young person or his or her counsel (subsection 8(5)).

- A review of an order made by a youth court judge who is not a judge of a superior county or district can be reviewed pursuant to sections 520 or 521 of the *Criminal Code.*

- For a review from an order made by a judge who is a judge of the superior, county or district court, the application must be made to a judge of the court of appeal: *Y.O.A.* section 8(6).

3

THE INITIAL INTERVIEW

3.1 GENERAL

○ In the initial interview, assume that your client has never had a lawyer before.

   ○ Explain that your job is to represent him or her and not the parent or guardian who may either be present, or paying the legal bills.

   ○ Explain to your client that your job is to follow his or her instructions, and not those of the parent or the family.

   ○ Explain that as a lawyer you are there to advise and inform your client of the various choices or decisions facing him or her, but that your client must always make the final decision.

   ○ Explain the concept of Solicitor-Client Privilege. Assure your client that you are duty bound as a lawyer not to discuss or disclose any information he or she gives you with anyone including his or her family, child care workers, teacher, friends or any other person and that the only way you will discuss the case with others is with your client's express consent.

   ○ If a parent or adult is present, it is good practice to ask your client if he or she prefers to have the parent remain during the initial part of the interview or whether he or she prefers to speak to you alone throughout the entire interview. Always speak to your client privately at some point. *Many lawyers routinely ask the parent or adult to leave when discussing the circumstances of the arrest or the offence, even when the client has expressed the desire to have the parent remain for the interview. It is important for the young person to see that you really do work for him or her and not the parent.*

3.2 INFORMATION TO OBTAIN

º During the initial interview, some very important information should be gathered. *While many of the areas of questioning may be similar when interviewing adults, some areas of concern are particular to the young person:*

1. Full Name

2. Age and Date of Birth

3. Address

    º Interview the client with an interest in finding a pattern in his or her living environment. It is not enough to just get a current address. Many youth move frequently between various group homes or facilities.

4. Phone Number

    º Determine if you can phone this number and leave a message. *Sometimes young persons wish to keep certain information from others who may share the phone.*

    º Determine if you can contact your client at school and obtain the phone number.

5. Birthplace

    º Determine the immigration status of your client if he or she is born outside of Canada.

6. Birth Parents

    º Be sensitive to the issue that some youth may have been adopted.

7. Primary Care Givers

   o Remember some youth have had people other than their parents raise them.

   o Obtain information and phone numbers about:

      o Children's Aid Society

      o Foster families

      o Relatives

8. Occupation of Parents or Supervising Adults

   o If parents are separated, how much contact does your client have with the parent with whom he or she does not reside.

   o Do both parents know about the charge?

   o Will your client allow you to call both parents?

9. Siblings

   o Names and ages.

   o Make discreet enquiries about siblings' criminal involvement.

10. School

   o Present grade and school.

   o Determine how long your client has attended the present school.

   o If your client has not been attending the present school for long, continue to question about past schools to obtain a pattern of the client's academic history.

- Is your client in special education, basic or advanced classes?

- Is your client passing any or all of the subjects?

- Is your client's attendance regular?

- Has your client ever been suspended for behaviourial problems?

- It is very important to establish with some clients whether they can read or write. *It may be important to ascertain the client's ability to read and comprehend if there is an issue about the admissibility of a statement.*

  - Do not assume that your client is literate just because your client attends school and appears to be promoted regularly.

  - Without embarrassing your client, ask him or her to read aloud something from a magazine or book.

  - Determine whether or not your client is aware of having any learning disabilities or attention difficulties. Ask whether or not any assessments have been done.

11. Employment

- Find out about summer jobs, part-time or full-time, volunteer work.

12. Outside Interests

13. Physical Health

14. Psychological Health

- Ask the client about his or her involvement with health care professionals. *A surprising number of young persons have been seen by social workers, or other child care workers.*

o Is your client on any psychotropic medication?

o Have the client and/or the parent or guardian authorized you to speak to any health care professionals involved by having them complete a direction or release form under the *Mental Health Act* (See *Appendix B, Form 4*).

15. Drug or Alcohol History

16. Youth Court Record

o If your client is on probation, obtain the name of the probation officer.

o If ordered by a court to complete community service or terms of probation, determine compliance.

o Seek your client's permission to contact probation officer, if necessary.

17. Outstanding Charges

o Determine the form of release.

o Determine your client's next court date and its purpose.

18. The Present Charges

o The release order.

   o Make a photocopy of any release form (i.e. summons, appearance notice, promise to appear, undertaking, recognizance).

   o Explain to the client that whatever the form of release, he or she is now on bail.

   o Explain the importance of complying with the release order especially if it requires the young person to appear at a later date for fingerprints.

- If the release is an undertaking or recognizance with conditions, explain the conditions to your client. Explain the importance of complying with the conditions and possible consequences if a condition is breached.

- Allegations Surrounding the Present Offence.

- Obtain the name of the co-accused, if any.

- Each lawyer has his or her own rules about asking questions regarding the current allegations on the first interview. For example, some lawyers obtain disclosure from the Crown and put the allegations to the client before getting the client's version. *This is a matter of personal preference and professional practice.*

- If it is your practice to explore the allegations before disclosure, see section 5.3.2 below which sets out a technique for interviewing the young person about statements made to the police or persons in authority. This is a crucial issue in acting for the young offenders.

3.3 ADVICE TO GIVE

3.3.1 RIGHT TO COUNSEL

- Advise that should your client be arrested or questioned in the future, he or she is to state that he or she has a lawyer and to give your name to the police.

- Explain to your client and family the right to remain silent and the right to counsel, in the simplest of terms. *Too often, young persons, especially, do not appreciate the rights in the standard police caution.*

- Advise your client that the police must serve his or her parents with a Notice to Parent pursuant to section 9 of the *Young Offenders Act*, even if your client does not want them notified. This means that the parent will find out about the charge.

º Advise your client of your office's procedure on accepting arrest calls from the client.

3.3.2 FIRST APPEARANCE

º If your client has never appeared in a court before, explain what will happen on his or her first appearance.

3.3.3 POSSIBLE OUTCOMES

º If you have discussed the allegations, you might want to briefly canvass possible outcomes with your client at this stage. See section 5.4 below.

º You might also want to advise your client about the alternative measures program, if one exists in your jurisdiction. See section 4.4 below.

3.3.4 BEHAVIOUR UNTIL TRIAL

º Discuss the importance of your client staying out of trouble until trial.

º This is especially important where a finding of guilt appears to be a possibility or where the charge is especially serious. See section 5.4 below.

3.3.5 COMMITTING THE STORY TO WRITING

º Where it becomes clear that your client will be giving evidence at trial, help your client preserve his or her memory by getting (where possible), at the earliest possible juncture, your client to reduce his or her entire story to writing.

º Get your client to put in writing everything he or she can remember about the day, including the clothes he or she was wearing and what he or she ate for breakfast. *Although irrelevant, your client's ability to refresh his or her*

memory with these details will ultimately help preserve memory of the entire day's events.

○ Get your client to write out in detail all dealings with the police, including treatment at the police station. You may discover a *Charter* violation.

3.4 A TALK WITH THE PARENTS

○ Remember that the right to instruct counsel is explicitly given to the young person, and an amendment to the *Young Offenders Act* was made to ensure that the right to instruct counsel was to be exercised by the young person personally.

○ If you are being retained by the parents of the young person, explain this feature of the legislation to parents at the first possible juncture. You will avoid uncomfortable conflict of interest problems. *Conflicts between the views of parents and the views of the client are all too commonplace.*

4

THE INITIAL APPEARANCE

4.1 GENERAL

4.1.1 TERMINOLOGY USED IN YOUTH COURT

○ Be aware from the initial appearance of the terminology specific to the world of the *Young Offenders Act.*

   ○ Refer to your client as the *"young person"*, never the *"young offender"*. Your client has not been found guilty of anything at this point.

   ○ If your client has a youth record, technically he has not been previously convicted of anything. Describe this situation by saying that there have been *"findings of guilt"* on previous charges.

   ○ Remember, previous findings of guilt do not result in sentences. The court rendered a *"disposition"*.

   ○ Note that under the *Young Offenders Act*, suspended sentences and conditional sentences do not exist.

   ○ When arguing the strength of the Crown's case at the bail hearing, remember that the Crown's case under the *Young Offenders Act* will never turn on the admissibility of a "confession". The correct terminology is *"statement"*, i.e. the Crown's case may depend upon the admissibility of the young person's "statement".

   ○ Where custody is a consideration, the disposing court will order a *predisposition report (PDR)*, not a pre-sentence report.

4.1.2 PROCEDURAL DIFFERENCES BETWEEN YOUTH AND ADULT COURT

○ Young offender trials do not differ significantly from adult provincial court trials. Certain basic differences between the juvenile and adult systems should be kept in mind, however:

    ○ Except in cases of first and second degree murder, there is no election of trial by jury if the Crown elects to proceed by indictment. As a consequence:

        ○ there is no preliminary hearing;

        ○ the Crown election affects the custodial disposition available and the length of time before a Youth Court record is destroyed.

    ○ In cases of first and second degree murder, the usual rules and procedures relating to election, preliminary inquiries and jury trials apply.

    ○ Special safeguards exist with respect to the admissibility of statements by young persons: *Y.O.A.* section 56.

    ○ The *Act* has its own specific range of dispositions: *Y.O.A.* section 20.

    ○ Section 24(1) and 24 (1.1) of the *Act* set out guidelines which must be considered before custody is ordered and section 24.1(4) lists factors to be considered when deciding whether open or secure custody should be ordered.

    ○ A parent cannot be excluded from the body of the court, even if the parent is a witness at trial: *Y.O.A.* section 39(2)(b).

    ○ Youth Court records must be destroyed within certain time parameters as set out in chapter 11.

º Dispositions are subject to review by the Youth Court during the course of the disposition if certain conditions are met, as discussed in chapter 10.

º The *Act* provides specfic protections for the privacy of the young person and sets limits on the disclosure of youth court records, as set out in sections 6.1.1, 6.1.2 and 11.5 of this book.

4.2 ESTABLISHING JURISDICTION

4.2.1 GENERAL

º A young person is defined as a person who is more than 12 years of age, but under the age of 18.

º This definition includes an adult who is alleged to have committed an offence while between the ages of 12 and 18.

º Subject to the transfer provisions, the youth court has exclusive jurisdiction to hear any matters involving *Criminal Code* charges against young persons.

  º As youth court has the powers and jurisdiction of a summary conviction court under the *Criminal Code*, a justice of the peace may preside over first appearance in certain jurisdictions. The youth court judge has the power to grant relief under the *Charter*.

4.2.2 DETERMINING WHETHER JURISDICTION HAS BEEN ESTABLISHED

º To determine whether jurisdiction over the offence and the young person has been gained by the court, the following questions must be addressed:

  º Has the correct age of the young person been established?

○ Note, jurisdiction is established by determining that the accused was a 'young person' within the meaning of the *Act* at the time of the offence. *The age of the young person at the time of appearance may not be relevant to establishing jurisdiction, he or she may be an adult at that time.*

○ Has notice to the parent been given?

　○ This can be established by evidence of oral notice, or proof of service of written notice: *Y.O.A.* section 9.

　○ The failure of the Crown to prove such notice where the young person has been detained pending first appearance does not render subsequent proceedings invalid: *Y.O.A.* section 9(8).

　○ Note, however, if a Notice to Appear or a summons has compelled the young person to attend the court, the failure to prove Notice to Parent, if not excused by the parent appearing (*Y.O.A.* section 9(*a*)) or dispensed with under the subsection, apparently renders any subsequent proceedings under the *Act* invalid. See *Smith v. R.* (1959), 124 C.C.C. 71 (S.C.C.).

○ Was the Information to be read to the young person on first appearance?

　○ The reading of the Information may be waived where the young person is represented by counsel.

　○ Note that the definition of 'counsel' in the *Criminal Code* does not include a student-at-law.

Although the *Young Offenders Act* mandates that the charge be read on first appearance, the Ontario Court of Appeal has ruled that the failure to do so is tantamount to an error in jurisdiction which can be cured by the application of section 485 of the *Criminal Code: R. v. B. (J.E.)* (June 7, 1993), Doc. CA C13406 (Ont. C.A.). The Queen's Bench in Manitoba has ruled similarly: *R. v. J. (J.T.)* (1986), 42 Man. R. (2d) 271, 28 C.C.C. (3d) 62. However, the Supreme Court of British Columbia has ruled that the failure to read the charge on first appearance is an error which prevents the court from ever assuming jurisdiction: *H. and R., Re* (1985), 21 C.C.C.

(3d) 396. Note, however, that the British Columbia decision predated amendments to section 485 (*Criminal Code*) aimed at curing losses of jurisdiction over both the offence and the person.

- Did the court inform the young person, if unrepresented, of his or her right to be represented by counsel?

  - The *Act* provides that if the young person wishes to obtain counsel, the court may order legal assistance from the provincial plan: *Y.O.A.* section 11(4)(b).

4.3 THE TRANSFER HEARING: EFFECT ON THE FIRST APPEARANCE

- Where the charge is likely to result in a transfer application determine as early as possible whether the Crown intends to apply for one.

- If a transfer hearing is likely, you must request a copy of the disclosure brief on the first appearance.

  - Put the request in writing.

  - This will help you plan your instructions to a psychological assessor carefully. Knowledge of the evidence against your client is essential to instructing any private psychological assessor. For example, if identification of the assailant is in issue, the assessor should not be asking your client questions about the offence, or else the assessor may be precluded (tactically) from giving evidence. The questions may uncover derivative evidence which could ultimately form part of the Crown's case at trial.

4.4 SEEKING ALTERNATIVE MEASURES

4.4.1 OVERVIEW

"Alternative Measures" refers to any system of diversion from the court process which is formalized by the Attorney General designation under section 4 of the *Young Offenders Act*.

4.4.2 PROCEDURE

- ° The programs vary from province to province. Most commonly, there is police involvement and a charge is laid (although some programs are pre-charge).

- ° Prior to first appearance or at first appearance, the case is recommended for diversion from the criminal process.

- ° Each jurisdiction has its own protocol for admission to the program. Familiarize yourself with the protocol. You may be able to offer creative solutions outside of the protocol in special cases.

- ° There is no constitutional requirement that a province have a program, or that there be consistency between jurisdictions: *R. v. S. (S.)*, [1990] 2 S.C.R. 254, 77 C.R. (3d) 273, 57 C.C.C. (3d) 115, and *R. v. S. (G.)*, [1990] 2 S.C.R. 294, 77 C.R. (3d) 303, 57 C.C.C. (3d) 92.

- ° In jurisdictions where diversion is post-charge and done after first appearance, use the first appearance to canvass the possibility of your client applying for the alternative measures program.

    - ° Request a protocol for the program approved by the Attorney General, prior to attending with your client. *Occasionally, local Crown practice may be more restrictive than the officially sanctioned program.*

    - ° *Appendix B, Form 5* is the form used in Ontario for requesting participation in this program.

4.4.3 WHEN TO CONSIDER THE ALTERNATIVE MEASURES PROGRAM

- ° Consider alternative measures if your client is prepared to accept responsibility for the offence as charged and does not want the matter to be heard by the youth court. The

Crown should also be prepared to consider alternative measures in this situation.

o Remember that programs and eligibility vary from jurisdiction to jurisdiction and from Crown to Crown.

o Inform your client of the following before assisting him or her with an application:

   o Whether or not a technical defence or other triable issue exists in the case, in spite of the young person's willingness to enter the program. *At first appearance, unfortunately, the total absence of any disclosure in most jurisdictions prevents many counsel from giving clients an accurate assessment of the chance of success where a technical defence exists.*

   o That the program is entirely voluntary.

   o That your client's admission of responsibility can never be used against him or her if the matter eventually proceeds to trial.

   o That your client can have counsel attend the alternative measure referral meeting (probation intake) with him or her. It is at this meeting that the particular 'measure' is negotiated.

      o Your client does not have to agree to any particular measure.

   o That your client has no right to a hearing or an appeal procedure if turned down for the program.

   o That the record of your client's participation in an alternative measures program is not destroyed until two years after the date on which your client consented to participate in the program.

   o That upon successful completion of an alternative measures program, the *Young Offenders Act* requires the youth court to *dismiss* the charge. Some jurisdictions will stay the charge upon entry into alternative measures.

4.4.4 DEVELOPMENTAL PROFILES

There is now an emerging body of Canadian social science literature which tends to demonstrate that young persons indeed need distinct assistance when dealing with the justice system. See *Appendix C*.

  ○ A developmental profile may be relevant when and if your client is being considered for alternative measures or the available diversion program in your jurisdiction.

5

PREPARATION FOR TRIAL

5.1 REVIEWING THE INFORMATION

○ Always request from the clerk of the court and receive a copy of the Information. *This is strongly suggested regardless of the offence facing the accused young person.*

○ Carefully review the Information for possible defects, for sufficiency, and other grounds for argument. *You may easily be throwing away a defence if you fail to do this.*

5.2 DISCLOSURE

5.2.1 REQUESTING DISCLOSURE FROM THE CROWN

○ Always request a copy of the disclosure material in writing except in the following circumstances:

　○ Where the client is charged with an offence such as failing to comply with various forms of release, wilfully breaching probation, failing to appear in court or for fingerprints, being unlawfully at large and escaping lawful custody etc.

　　○ These offences are proven by, among other things, the Crown establishing that the proper documentation was given to the accused. The officer-in-charge or the prosecutor may vet the file before the trial in order to comply with the obligation to provide you with full disclosure in response to your request. *This may be detrimental to your case as it may give the opposing party the opportunity to discover that certain documents are missing and obtain them before trial.*

○ In all other cases, ordering disclosure in a timely fashion is tremendously important.

○ Except for cases of murder, charges dealt with under the *Young Offenders Act*, unless transferred to adult court, do not have a preliminary inquiry. You must, therefore, be prepared to proceed with the trial, and the first part of preparation is receiving full disclosure.

○ If charges are serious, a transfer application by the Crown may be likely. Full disclosure is essential to being able to instruct a private assessor. See section 8.1.2 below.

○ Be thorough and creative in deciding which documents, records, reports or statements you will request the Crown to produce. *The fact that the Supreme Court of Canada in R. v. Stinchcombe*, [1991] 3 S.C.R. 326, 8 C.R. (4th) 277, 68 C.C.C. (3d) 1, has changed the way Crown attorneys give disclosure does not mean that the Crown will necessarily think of all documents the defence may need. The Crown is not privy to the defence's case plan.

○ Note, the Crown or police may not have all of the relevant documentation in their control. *For example, the alleged victims of youth crime are often other youth. Prior contact with social services by victims or witnesses may have generated documentation which is relevant and helpful to mounting a defence. Further, in certain types of cases, Crowns may feel legally bound to avoid exposing themselves to materials which may have a statutory or other privilege which attaches. This is because the victim or witness or complainant may want to advance some privilege and have a trial court curtail disclosure to the defence.*

○ If there is relevant documentation controlled by parties other than the police and Crown, determine the correct procedure for its release or disclosure. Examples of such documentation may be:

o Mental health or psychological records which have been generated in provincial facilities and reside with the Records Department of the particular institution. These documents are almost always covered by provincial legislation concerning their release.

o Group home logs and progress reports. These documents may be in the possession of the Children's Aid, or they may be in the possession of the group home itself. A phone call usually reveals the name of the proper party to subpoena.

o School Records. These documents are usually at the young person's last school. These documents are almost always subject to provincial legislation.

There is a line of cases developing concerning production of these types of 'privileged' documents. Courts are recognizing the complainant's right to privacy in certain cases, notably sexual assaults. Where the complainant's records are the subject of subpoena, some courts are requiring counsel to demonstrate that there is information that is likely to be material in the proceeding in the documents under subpoena (section 698(1) *Criminal Code*) before production of the documents is ordered. In adult cases, you have the opportunity to establish the existence of such information during the preliminary inquiry. But the situation is obviously different under the *Young Offenders Act* where there is no preliminary inquiry. You are advised, when seeking disclosure, to make a motion to the trial court for production (see *Appendix B, Form 6* for a sample of a Notice of Motion used for this purpose). Be prepared, within the sanctuary of a *voir dire*, to establish the existence of certain documentation and its materiality to an issue in the trial. For a detailed analysis of these issues, refer to: Lee Mitchell, *Production of Private Records in Criminal Cases* (Toronto: Carswell, 1997).

5.3 SPECIAL RULES OF EVIDENCE AND PREPARING FOR THE *VOIR DIRE*

5.3.1 SECTION 56 OF THE *YOUNG OFFENDERS ACT*

Although the *Young Offenders Act* adopts generally the law relating to the admissibility of statements, rules particular to young persons are enshrined in section 56.

o Familiarize yourself with section 56 before interviewing your client. Under this section:

- A statement must be voluntary.

- Young persons have a right to know their rights in language they understand.

- These rights include the right to silence and the right to know that statements can be used in court.

- The right to consult with counsel *and* an adult person and to have them present when making a statement are mandated.

- A young person who does not wish to exercise his or her rights must waive them on videotape or in writing if the statement is to be admissible.

- "Spontaneous" statements made to police or persons in authority are admissible if made before the authority could comply with the section 56 rights advice.

- Where a young person has held themselves out to be aged 18 or older, the statement may be admissible.

- Where the young person has been held for any length of time at the police station, you should assume that a statement was taken. You can verify this through disclosure. *Young people are notorious for being uncertain as to which legal proceedings have been brought to bear. For example, many young people think that the first appearance is for trial purposes.*

5.3.2 TECHNIQUE FOR INTERVIEWING CLIENT ABOUT STATEMENT

The following is a method for interviewing your client to determine whether a statement was given and if the statement is admissible pursuant to section 56 and the common law test of admissibility:

(a) The Arrest

- Begin by asking your client:

  - Where were you when the police came to arrest you?

  - Who was with you?

  - If your client was at home, where were his or her parents or adult family members?

  - At what time did the police arrive?

  - How many police officers arrived?

  - Were they uniformed or plain clothed?

  - Did the police identify themselves?

  - Did you say anything to the police before they started talking?

  - Did they tell you why they were there?

    - Did you understand?

  - Did the police begin to ask you about the offence?

  - Did you answer the questions?

    - If so, what did you say?

    - Who was present?

  - Did the police arrest you?

    - What did they say?

    - Did you understand?

    - Did you understand what it meant to have the "right to retain and instruct counsel"?

39

○ Did you understand the right to remain silent?

○ What did you say?

○ Did the police offer you the use of a telephone?

○ Did the police search you?

  ○ Did the police search you before or after they arrested you?

○ Did the police search your room, car or locker?

  ○ If so, who gave the police permission?

○ How did you feel when the police came to arrest you?

  ○ Were you nervous, scared or intimidated?

(b) The Trip to the Station

○ If the police took your client to the police station after they made the arrest, ask your client the following:

○ Were you handcuffed?

  ○ How did you feel?

○ Did the police advise your parents where you were going and why?

  ○ Did your parents express a concern about going with you to the police station?

  ○ What did the police tell your parents?

  ○ Did you want your parents to go with you?

  ○ If so, did you do or say anything?

o During the ride to the police station, did the police say anything to you?

  o What did you say?

  o How did you feel?

o Did you go straight to the police station?

(c) Events at the Station

(i) The Booking Procedure

o Once at the police station, your client would have been booked in through a desk sergeant or other police official who might have again advised your client as to his or her rights. Ask the client the following:

  o What time did you arrive at the station?

  o Did you understand what the police officer was telling you?

  o Did you want to call a lawyer?

    o If so, did you know how to contact a lawyer?

  o Had you ever had a lawyer before?

  o Did the police offer you a telephone?

  o Did they tell you about duty counsel?

  o Did you know what a duty counsel was or how they might help you?

(ii) The Interview Room at the Station

o In the police station, the young person may be taken to an interview room, and the following questions might be helpful in eliciting what took place there:

    ○ What did the room look like?

    ○ Were there any windows, any toilet facilities, a tele-phone?

    ○ What time did you enter the room?

    ○ Were you in the room alone for a period of time?

      ○ If so, how long?

    ○ How did you feel?

    ○ When the police returned, how many police officers came in the room?

    ○ Were they the same officers who arrested you?

    ○ How long were you in the room before the police came in?

    ○ Were you hungry or thirsty?

      ○ Did you make any requests?

      ○ If not, why not?

    ○ Did you need to use the washroom?

(iii) Giving the Statement

    ○ You have, at this point, established that police were in the interview room with your client. In these circumstances, it would appear that the taking of a statement is imminent:

      ○ Did the police have a typewriter or any recording device like a taperecorder or video machine?

      ○ Did the police identify themselves?

o Did the police begin by asking questions about the alleged offence?

o Did you answer the questions?

o Did the police ask the following questions? *The aim of this inquiry is to determine compliance with section 56 of the Young Offenders Act.*

  o Do you understand the offence with which you are charged?

  o Do you wish to speak to a lawyer?

  o Do you wish a lawyer to be present during the interview?

  o Do you wish to speak to a parent?

  o Do you wish your parent to be present?

  o If a parent is not available, do you wish to speak to an adult or an adult relative?

  o Do you wish to have the adult relative present?

  o If an adult relative is not available, do you wish to speak to another adult?

  o Do you wish to have an adult present?

o If the answer to all these questions was "no", why did you not wish to speak to any of these people?

o Did the police ask you to sign a paper?

o Was the paper your statement?

o Why did you sign the paper?

  o Did the police tell you to sign the paper?

43

- If so, what did they say?

- Did the police repeat the primary and secondary caution?

  - Did they tell you that you had the right to remain silent?

    - Did they tell you that if any other police officer had said anything to induce you to give a statement that you should not rely on that promise or threat?

- In what language was this told to you?

- Did you understand this?

- Ask the client to explain the right to you.

- How were you feeling?

- Did you feel like you had a choice as to whether you gave the statement?

- Did the police promise you anything if you gave the statement? (*e.g.* a release, to go easy on you at the trial.)

- Did the police threaten you or hurt you in order to force you to give the statement?

  - Are there any injuries to be photographed or noted?

(iv) The Statement Itself

- Once you understand the preliminaries which lead to the taking of the statement, ask about the statement itself:

  - Who was present in the room?

  - Did the police hand-write the statement or did you write it yourself?

  - Was it tape recorded or video taped?

○ What questions were asked and what answers did you give?

○ Did you sign the statement?

○ Did you read the statement before you signed it?

○ Did you initial any changes to the statement?

   ○ If so, why?

○ How long did the statement take?

(v) The Form of Release

○ Determine whether at the conclusion of the process of taking the statement, the police:

   ○ released your client from the police station on a promise to appear or on an undertaking before a justice of the peace; or

   ○ held your client for a show cause hearing?

5.3.3 OTHER EVIDENCE REGARDING ADMISSIBILITY OF STATEMENT

○ Interview other persons who were present when your client was arrested, taken from the home or school, or interviewed at the police station.

○ Speak to any person who received the Notice to Parent or a telephone call from police while the child was at the police station.

   ○ Find out what they were told or understood the process would be.

   ○ Find out at what time they were called.

5.3.4 A NOTE ON CASE LAW INTERPRETING SECTION 56

º When preparing for a *voir dire*, you should keep in mind some of the following judicial interpretations of section 56:

   º The protection of the section does not apply to a young person who makes a statement after he turns 18: *R. v. Z. (D.A.)*, [1992] 2 S.C.R. 1025, 16 C.R. (4th) 133, 76 C.C.C. (3d) 97.

   º Statements made by young persons *suspected* of committing an offence are also protected by the section: *R. v. J. (J.T.)*, [1990] 2 S.C.R. 755, [1990] 6 W.W.R. 152, 59 C.C.C. (3d) 1. But statements made during police investigations before the young person is a suspect may not be so protected.

   º Where the content of the statement forms the *actus reus* of the offence (public mischief, obstruction of justice, threatening), section 56 protections do not apply: *R. v. J. (J.)* (1988), 65 C.R. (3d) 371, 29 O.A.C. 104, 43 C.C.C. (3d) 257 (C.A.).

   º Parents are not necessarily persons in authority unless there is some connection between the decision to call the authorities and the inducement to the young person to make a statement: *R. v. B. (A.)* (1986), 50 C.R. (3d) 247, 13 O.A.C. 68, 26 C.C.C. (3d) 17 (C.A.).

   º Once the young person tells the police that he or she wants a parent or other adult present, the right arises to have that request implemented immediately before there is further questioning: *R. v. P. (S.)* (1991), 44 O.A.C. 316 (C.A.).

   º Once the police or authority figure have commenced questioning the youth, any utterances by the youth are not "spontaneous": *R. v. J. (J.T.)*, [1990] 2 S.C.R. 755, 79 C.R. (3d) 219, 59 C.C.C. (3d) 1.

○ "Statements" include gestures and evidence obtained as part of the statement such as during a "re-enactment" of the offence: *R. v. J. (J.T.)*, [1990] 2 S.C.R. 755, 79 C.R. (3d) 219, 59 C.C.C. (3d) 1.

○ A person who stands *in loco parentis* such as a foster parent is a "person in authority" under section 56: *R. v. A. (M.)* (August 16, 1994), Doc. Quesnel 944 (B.C. Prov. Ct.)

○ A statement taken after an inadmissible statement may be inadmissible as "tainted" by the first statement where the subsequent statement is close in time to the first, is a continuation of the first and the initial statement substantially influenced the making of the second statement — even where there is compliance with section 56 before the second or subsequent statement: *R. v. I. (L.R.)*, [1993] 4 S.C.R. 504, 26 C.R. (4th) 119, 86 C.C.C. (3d) 289.

5.4 DISCUSSING POSSIBLE OUTCOMES

Some young people may be unfamiliar with the court system. Others may know less than they think. It is important to advise the client about possible outcomes. This is most easily done after disclosure. However, you might have already introduced this topic in your initial interview.

○ Each case must be assessed individually.

○ In cases where the outcome is evident or the charge serious, discuss the possible outcome of the case and, most importantly, the fact that the young person's behaviour pending the trial will be of major importance.

○ Advise that your client's conduct in school, at home and in the community may significantly influence a judge's final disposition of the case. *Each jurisdiction is different, but depending on the length of the delay in coming to trial, your client may be able to radically improve his or her overall performance. This, of course, will weigh positively in his or her favour at the time of disposition.*

o If your client is charged with very minor offence, he or she should be assured that it is unlikely that there will be a custodial disposition.

6

THE TRIAL

The actual trial of a young offender does not differ significantly from adult provincial court trial. The following, however, are of particular relevance in the trials of young people:

6.1 PROVISIONS PROTECTING THE PRIVACY OF THE YOUNG OFFENDER

6.1.1 PUBLICATION BANS

- Remember, section 38(1) of the *Act* prohibits the publication of the name of a young offender who has committed or is alleged to have committed an offence. It also protects any child or young person who appears as a witness in connection with the offence.

The overall prohibition against identifying young persons is subject to certain exceptions:

- Through court order, for the purposes of apprehending a dangerous young person.

- Disclosure by a provincial director or youth court worker for the purposes of preparing a report.

- With a court order, to prevent harm to a particular person or persons at risk.

- Disclosure to persons engaged in the supervision or care of young persons, including school board personnel by the provincial director, the police or other persons supervising youth where necessary:

○ to ensure compliance by the young person with bail, probation and other specified orders; or

○ to ensure the safety of staff, students or others.

Any person to whom information is disclosed is bound by specific provisions relating to disclosure and destruction of information: section 38 (1.12; 1.14; 1.15.)

6.1.2 EXCLUSION OF THE PUBLIC FROM THE PROCEEDING

○ Note, that under section 39 of the *Act*, any person whose presence is unnecessary to the proceeding may be excluded from all or part of the trial if:

○ any evidence or information presented would seriously injure the young offender or any child who is a witness in the proceeding or the victim of the offence; or

○ the exclusion would be in the interest of public morals, the maintenance of order or the proper administration of justice.

○ The *Act* specifically prohibits the exclusion of the parent of the young person or any adult assisting him or her.

6.2 USING SOCIAL SCIENCE LITERATURE IN ARGUMENT

○ Consider raising the special attributes of young persons where circumstances allow.

○ There is, for example, an emerging body of Canadian social science literature which tends to demonstrate that young persons need distinct assistance when dealing with the justice system. See *Appendix C. Your client's particular profile, coupled with the literature on the developmental profile of youth, could provide fertile ground for argument when considering, on voir dire, whether or not the young person understood what rights he or she may have been waiving when making a statement at the police station.*

7

MEDICAL AND PSYCHOLOGICAL REPORTS/FITNESS AND SANITY

7.1 OVERVIEW OF LEGISLATION

On February 4, 1992, Bill C-20 was proclaimed bringing sweeping changes to the law relating to mentally disordered accused. These amendments became Part XX of the *Criminal Code*, and the majority of the provisions were incorporated into the *Young Offenders Act*.

7.2 SECTION 13

7.2.1 THE LEGISLATION

- Section 13 remains the section to be used to order an assessment for the non-mentally disordered young person or where the young person has some emotional problem.

- A medical, psychological or psychiatric report may be ordered pursuant to section 13 either on the consent of the young person and prosecutor (section 13 (1)(*a*)) or on a motion by the court, the young person or the prosecutor where there are reasonable grounds to believe that:

  - the young person may be suffering from a physical or mental illness or disorder;

  - a psychological disturbance;

  - an emotional disturbance;

  - a learning disability; or

  - mental disability: section 13 (1)(*b*).

○ A section 13 report can only be ordered for purposes of:

  ○ considering a transfer application under section 16: section 13(2)(*a*);

  ○ making or reviewing a disposition under the *Young Offenders Act*: section 13(2)(*b*);

  ○ making an application for continued custody to determine whether a young person should be held until the end of the disposition as opposed to being placed under conditional supervision pursuant to section 26.1(1): section 13(2)(*c*);

  ○ setting the discretionary terms of a conditional supervision order under section 26.2(1): section 13(2)(*d*);

  ○ ordering disposition under section 26.6(2) after a breach of a conditional supervision order: section 13(2)(*e*);

  ○ determining whether the young person poses a risk such that disclosure of information is necessary to prevent harm to someone under section 38(1.5): section 13(2)(*f*).

○ A section 13 report cannot be ordered to determine if the young person is unfit to stand trial or was not criminally responsible by reason of mental disorder.

○ The amendments to section 13 ensure that the non-mentally disordered young person has the same level of protection as has been added to the *Young Offenders Act* for the mentally disordered youth.

○ There is the presumption against the detention of the young person while the report is being prepared: section 13(3.1), and any remand into custody cannot be for more than 30 days: section 13(3).

7.2.2 REQUESTING OR CONSENTING TO A SECTION 13 ASSESSMENT

○ Always carefully consider whether requesting or consenting to a section 13 court ordered assessment is a good idea.

  ○ It is always in your client's interest to control the admission of psychiatric evidence.

  ○ Canvass with the client and his or her family, their ability to pay for a private, hence, controlled assessment.

  ○ If you are retained by legal aid authorities, consider writing for authorization to retain a private assessment.

  ○ Canvass the availability of assessment facilities for your client's age group. The option of an out-patient assessment may bear on your client's willingness to be assessed. If there are no funded assessment options for your client you may wish to consider a challenge to an "uninformed" disposition.

7.2.3 THE TRANSFER APPLICATION AND THE SECTION 13 ASSESSMENT

On an application to transfer, a section 13 assessment may be very helpful to the Crown. If the assessment reveals that the young person requires treatment in excess of that available as a disposition in youth court, or whether the prognosis for the successful treatment of a youth within a three (to ten) year period is either unlikely or unpredictable, this fact is to be given considerable weight in assessing whether the interests of society are better served by the transfer of a youth to ordinary court. See *R. v. R. (S.)* (1991), 1 O.R. (3d) 785, 44 O.A.C. 76 (C.A.) at pp. 788-789 (O.R.); *R. v. R. (M.)* (January 16, 1991), Doc. CA 869/90 (Ont. C.A.), leave to appeal to S.C.C. refused (1991), 50 O.A.C. 159 (note), 136 N.R. 415 (note); *R. v. B. (B.A.)* (December 27, 1989), Doc. Toronto RE 2070/89 (Ont. H.C.), affirmed (September 21, 1990), Doc. No. CA 68/90 (Ont. C.A.).

○ A Crown seeking a section 13 assessment for purposes of a transfer application will have to prove on reasonable grounds that the young person may be suffering from a disorder.

○ Note, however, the very fact that a young person has committed murder may provide the reasonable grounds for a youth court judge to make his or her own motion for a section 13 assessment: *R. v. S. (G.)* (1991), 5 O.R. (3d) 97, 50 O.A.C. 163 (C.A.), leave to appeal to S.C.C. refused (1992), 6 O.R. (3d) xiii (note), 137 N.R. 398 (note), 55 O.A.C. 400 (note) (S.C.C.).

○ Before responding on the issue of a section 13 assessment for purposes of a transfer, review Chapter 8 on Transfer Applications.

○ Get as much disclosure as possible and be totally familiar with your client's case.

○ There are many issues which may arise and of which you should be aware:

  ○ Any statement made by the young person during the section 13 assessment is admissible against him or her to challenge credibility in any proceeding where his or her testimony is materially inconsistent with his or her earlier statements: subsection 13.1(2)(*f*).

  ○ If identity of the accused is an issue at trial, obtain from the judge ordering the assessment strict guidelines delineating the areas about which the examiner is permitted to question the young person.

○ In some situations, a section 13 assessment which reveals your client's insight and remorse may be useful.

○ If you are satisfied that there is an overwhelmingly strong case against your client and a finding of guilt is imminent, then your client's cooperation with the section 13 assessment may be beneficial.

○ However, in many more situations, you should carefully consider whether participating in the section 13 assessment will be of any benefit to him or her at all.

7.3 SECTION 13.2: THE MENTALLY DISORDERED YOUNG PERSON

7.3.1 THE LEGISLATION

° Subject to a few exceptions, section 13.2 incorporates the amendments to the *Criminal Code* pertaining to mentally disordered accused.

° Jane Arnup in her paper, *"The Mental Disorder Amendments; Impact on Young Persons"*, prepared for the Canadian Bar Association Continuing Legal Education program for November 14, 1992, cites several examples of differences between the adult and young offender provisions for the mentally disordered accused:

  ° Hospital orders are not available for young persons; thus, the provision of the Bill pertaining to adults which would determine whether a hospital order should be made has been excluded from the *Young Offenders Act.*

  ° The provisions relating to dangerous mentally disordered accused do not apply to young persons.

  ° The notice provisions have been modified to conform to the standard notice provisions for young persons, including notice to parents (section 13.2(2)) and the consequences for the failure to comply with the notice provisions: sections 13.2(3) and (4).

  ° Similarly, the parents of the young person must be given an opportunity to make any submissions to the court or Review Board before a mental disorder disposition is imposed: section 13.2(6).

  ° Caps for young persons are the maximum period for which the young person could be detained had the young person been convicted.

  ° After a finding of unfitness, the Crown must return to court every year to demonstrate that it still has a *prima facie* case against the young person if the young person is still unfit. For adults, this finding of the *prima facie* case must be made every two years.

○ Subsection 13.2(8) and (9) apply where the young person is found unfit to stand trial after a transfer application has been made. Here the Attorney General can make application to have the cap, which would otherwise apply, raised to the cap which an adult would face under similar conditions.

○ Subsection 13.2(11) indicates that a hospital refers to a place of treatment, custody or assessment for young persons.

7.4 DIVERSION OF YOUNG PERSONS WITH A MENTAL ILLNESS

○ Your province may have a diversion protocol in place for persons with mental illness or other related disabilities. Determine whether or not the protocol applies to young persons and whether or not your client fits the profile and is willing to be diverted from the criminal justice stream to the mental health or children's services stream.

8

TRANSFER APPLICATIONS

8.1 THE APPLICATION

8.1.1 OVERVIEW

The decision to proceed in adult court is the most serious consequence provided by the *Young Offenders Act*. Once transferred, the youth faces the entire panoply of sentences available, most importantly, ''life'' for murder and manslaughter. These particular sentences faced in adult court by the youth are ameliorated only by the reduced parole ineligibility periods which must be set by the sentencing court.

- ° The seriousness of the consequences of this application should lead you to consider sending the brief to very experienced counsel as soon as the likelihood of a transfer application arises.

8.1.2 THE STATUTORY TEST

- ° Transfer applications are governed by sections 16, 16.1 and 16.2 of the *Young Offenders Act*. Sentencing in adult court after a conviction on first or second degree murder is governed by sections 745.1 and 745.3 of the *Criminal Code*.

- ° Section 16 sets out the parameters regarding proceeding in or transfer to adult court. Youth aged 16 or 17 at the time of the offence are to be proceeded against in adult court for the offences of:

  - ° first or second degree murder

  - ° attempt murder

  - ° manslaughter

○ aggravated sexual assault

○ This automatic "transfer" is subject to an order of the youth court, on application of the Crown, or of the young person, that the youth be dealt with in youth court. The *Act* does not specify when such an application may be made. Thus it may be open to defence counsel to bring the application following the preliminary inquiry in adult court.

○ The *Act* specifies that the application is to be made orally in the presence of the other party, or in writing on notice to the other party. The opposing party must then file a notice of opposition, failing which the court must order the youth dealt with in youth court. If the other party (usually the Crown) is in agreement with the "transfer down" to youth court, he or she should file a notice of non-opposition. The result of the latter notice is an order that the matter be dealt with in youth court. The timing for the hearing or order is within 21 days of the notice to the other party, subject to the consent of both parties. For a precedent for a Notice of Application for a "transfer down" hearing, see *Appendix B, Form 10.*

○ For all offences other than those noted above, there remains a presumption that the youth will be dealt with in youth court unless:

   ○ the youth was 14 at the time of the offence charged; and

   ○ is charged with an indictable offence other than those offences over which the provincial court has absolute jurisdiction (section 553 of the *Code*); and

   ○ the young person or crown applies for and is successful in obtaining an order that the matter proceed in ordinary court.

○ An application for transfer to adult court can be made after the information is laid and at any time before the adjudication of the matter. The guidelines relating to notices and

timing in "transfer down" applications do not appear to
apply.

It may seem odd that a young person would apply for transfer to ordinary court;
however in some instances and in some jurisdictions, the penalties given to adults
will be less substantial than those given to youth. This may be particularly true of
soliciting offences. Nonetheless, caution is urged when considering recommending
a transfer to adult court. A thorough submission on disposition in youth court may
be more beneficial to the young person in terms of the overall risks associated with
being in the adult system. Note that a youth convicted in adult court can serve time
in a youth facility (see section 8.3 below): *Y.O.A.* section 16.2.

- Section 16 sets the test for the court deciding the transfer
  or "transfer down" application: where protection of the public and rehabilitation of the young person cannot be reconciled by trying the young person in youth court, then
  protection of the public becomes the paramount consideration. In such a case, the young person shall be dealt
  with in ordinary court.

- The onus rests with the applicant.

- The court *shall* take into consideration:

  - The nature and seriousness of the alleged offence.

    - In this regard, the court is entitled (not mandated) to
      decide the matter taking the Crown's case at its most
      damaging to the accused.

    - The test for admissibility of hearsay evidence for the
      purpose of establishing the facts seems to be that the
      evidence is capable of belief and not merely trifling in
      nature: *R v. S. (G.)* (1991), 5 O.R. (3d) 97, 50 O.A.C.
      163 (C.A.), leave to appeal to S.C.C. refused: (1992),
      6 O.R. (3d) xiii (note), 137 N.R. 398 (note), 55 O.A.C.
      400 (note) (S.C.C.).

    - You should consider making application to cross-ex-
      amine the sources of the hearsay evidence: *R. v. H.
      (C.)* (1986), 1 W.C.B. (2d) 59 (Ont. Prov. Ct.).

o Age, maturity and background of the young person and the young person's criminal or youth court record.

o The adequacy of the *Young Offenders Act* as compared to the *Criminal Code* or other Acts of Parliament.

  o This plank of the test usually means: Is the disposition of five years in the *Young Offenders Act* adequate to protect society?

  o The Saskatchewan Court of Appeal has held that the onus is on the Crown to establish that protection of the public requires more time than is available under the *Young Offenders Act. R. v. H. (E.E.)* (1987), 57 C.R. (3d) 29, 35 C.C.C. (3d) 67 (Sask. C.A.).

o The availability of treatment or correctional resources.

  o This part of the test is of reduced importance now that the *Act* has been amended to allow the adult sentencing court to send a young person back to the youth system to serve part of his or her sentence, even though tried as an adult.

  o Be prepared to call evidence from custodial programmers working in the youth system as to the effect of having to design a program for a young person facing life imprisonment who will only be in that system for three years or so. *Programs in youth centres are based on Y.O.A. maximum sentences and custodial programmers may find it difficult to take a young person whom they are simply preparing for an adult facility. As well, there is the effect of such programming on other young offenders.*

o This argument should be made the subject of evidence, if possible. *This is to counter the argument of the Crown that the availability of keeping the transferred youth in the youth custody system for a period at the beginning of the sentence lessens the impact of transfer.*

- Before making a decision to transfer, the court must consider a pre-disposition report;

  - submissions of young person or counsel;

  - any other factors considered relevant by court.

8.1.3 THE ONUS OF PROOF

- The onus of justifying a transfer remains throughout the proceeding with the applicant: *R. v. M. (S.H.)*, [1989] 2 S.C.R. 446, 71 C.R. (3d) 257, 50 C.C.C. (3d) 503: *Y.O.A.* section 16(1.11).

8.1.4 ACTING ON A TRANSFER APPLICATION

- Because the consequences of a transfer application are so serious, the approach taken by you should be ardent in acting on this kind of application.

- Contact counsel who have done such an application in the same jurisdiction. *This is a very important step.*

  - Each province has very different custodial approaches. These are the subject matter of evidence. Someone familiar with the system through direct experience or because of a previous transfer hearing should be contacted so that counsel has an overview of the jurisdiction's resources.

  - Several provinces have official child advocates who can be a valuable asset in terms of accessing and identifying resources in the youth system. Refer to *Appendix D* for a list of child advocates across Canada.

  - The *Act* and the case law in themselves provide few clues as to the character of evidence which must be called.

° On *very* serious offences (*e.g.* murder), there is nothing to lose by vigorously resisting transfer.

   ° As an appeal by the unsuccessful party is almost automatic, an incomplete hearing, or one with sloppy evidence ties the hands of appellate counsel working with the transcript. *Fresh evidence at the appeal stage may be received by the court, but the test for admission is unclear: R. v. S. (G.)* (1991), 5 O.R. (3d) 97, 50 O.A.C. 163 (C.A.), leave to appeal to S.C.C. refused (1992), 6 O.R. (3d) xiii (note), 137 N.R. 398 (note), 55 O.A.C. 400 (note) (S.C.C.).

° Where the charge against your client is likely to result in a transfer application, determine as early as possible whether the Crown intends to proceed in this fashion.

   ° Knowing that a transfer hearing is intended will influence your approach at the bail hearing.

   ° Whether in adult court prior to a "transfer down" hearing or in youth court, use the bail hearing to thoroughly cross-examine the officer or detective who prepared the Crown's synopsis of the case. *This is a free practice run at the officer-in-charge who will certainly be called at the transfer hearing to state the allegations.*

° On the *first* appearance, request a copy of the disclosure brief.

   ° Put the request in writing.

° Knowledge of the evidence against the accused is essential to instructing any private psychological assessor. *If, for example, identification of the assailant is in issue, the assessor should not ask your client any questions about the offence, or else the assessor may be precluded (tactically) from giving evidence. A probing of your client may uncover derivative evidence which could ultimately form part of the Crown's case at trial.*

○ Always plan the instructions you give to your assessor very carefully. *It may be that you only wish to assess your client for maturity and presence of remorse. Some assessors are prepared to do this on the basis of a personality inventory test alone.*

○ If psychological or mental fitness is an issue, see section 6.1.1(*c*).

8.2 DETENTION PENDING TRIAL — SECTION 16.1

○ There is a statutory presumption that persons under the age of 18 in detention awaiting the outcome of a trial in adult court shall be housed in a young offenders facility, unless the court is of the opinion it would be in the best interest of the young person and for the safety of others to move the young person to an adult facility.

○ There is an opposite rebuttable presumption where the young person is over the age of 18 at the time of trial in the adult court.

8.3 PLACEMENT AFTER CONVICTION IN ADULT COURT — SECTION 16.2

○ Once the convicted young person is sentenced in adult court, the sentencing court must make an order which places the young person in a young offenders facility, a provincial facility, or where the sentence is for two or more years, a penitentiary: *R. v. R. (A.)* (1993), 81 C.C.C. (3d) 436 (Ont. Prov. Div.), affirmed (March 18, 1996), Doc. CA C15368 (Ont. C.A.).

○ The parties and the provincial and federal correctional systems have the right to be heard.

○ The court is obliged to hear evidence on:

○ the safety of the young person;

- o the safety of the public;

- o young person's accessibility to family;

- o the safety of other inmates;

- o whether the young person would be a negative role model for other youth;

- o the young person's maturity;

- o the availability of resources in different custodial systems;

- o past behaviour in custody;

- o recommendations of representatives of different custodial systems;

- o any other factor the court considers relevant.

- o The Court shall order a report be prepared.

- o On application later, the original order of custodial placement may be changed if circumstances change materially.

9

DISPOSITIONS OF THE COURT

9.1 PLEA AND FINDING OF GUILT

If a plea of 'not guilty' is entered, or where the youth court is not satisfied that the facts relied upon by the prosecution support a plea of 'guilty' on the stated charge, then the court is bound by section 19 of the *Young Offenders Act* to proceed to try the matter. In youth court, there is technically no conviction: there is a finding of guilt or a dismissal of charges.

9.2 AVAILABLE DISPOSITIONS

Once there has been a finding of guilt, the court has an array of options available to it for the purposes of making a disposition. *Under the Young Offenders Act, the court disposes of the matter; in adult court there would be a sentencing of the convicted person.*

9.2.1 CUSTODIAL SENTENCES

(a) Custodial Ranges

- There are four custodial ranges available to a disposing court:

  - Custody to be served intermittently or continuously, two years from the date of committal for most offences.

  - Custody to be served intermittently or continuously, three years from the date of committal where an adult would face imprisonment for life for the same offence (such as break and enter).

  - Custody to be served continuously for up to six years, and then subject to conditional supervision for up to four years where the young person has been found guilty of first degree murder.

o Custody to be served continuously for up to four years, followed by up to three years of conditional supervision in the case of second degree murder.

o Note that in cases of first and second degree murder, the Crown attorney can apply to have the young person continue in custody as opposed to being released under supervision: *Y.O.A.* section 26.1.

(b) Level of Custody

o There are two types of custody available:

o open
o secure.

Both types of custody are defined in section 24.1 of the *Act*. The court must specify to which type of custody, open or secure, the young person is committed. This is called deciding 'level' of custody. The provincial director will decide *where* the young person will be committed within the facilities designated by the province for the 'level' of custody ordered. In some provinces the provincial director may have the power to decide the ''level'' of custody. In most provinces, this power still rests with the youth court judge.

(c) When Custody is Appropriate

(i) Guidelines From the *Act*

o The *Young Offenders Act* sets out specific guidelines which must be followed by the court when deciding whether or not custody is the appropriate disposition. The court must consider the following:

o that custody is not to be used as a substitute for child protection, health and other social measures;

o that offences which do not involve personal injury should not generally attract a custodial disposition;

- that custody shall be a last resort when all reasonable, available alternatives have been canvassed.

- Subject to waiver by the parties, the court must consider a pre-disposition report.

- The court must provide reasons setting out why dispositions other than a custodial disposition were not adequate.

Note that the option of a conditional sentence provided for in the *Criminal Code* (section 742.1) is not available in youth court as an alternative to a custodial disposition. While it may be possible to fashion such an outcome by virtue of section 20.(1) or through a probation order (section 23), you may wish to consider a constitutional challenge to the lack of this option to persons under the age of 18.

- The *Act* also provides guidance with respect to level of custody. The Youth Court or the provincial director must take into account:

  - that the least intrusive level be utilized, having regard to:

  - the nature and seriousness of the offence;

  - the needs/circumstances of the young person including proximity to family, school, job and support services;

  - the safety of other youth;

  - the interests of society;

  - that the level of custody should allow for the best match of programs to meet the young person's needs and behaviours, and considering any reports;

  - the likelihood of escape if in open custody;

  - the recommendations of the youth court or provincial director.

(d) Location Where Custodial Sentence to be Served

º Where custody is a certainty, or a good possibility, you should be aware of the fact that the place your client is eventually placed may be of some importance. *In some jurisdictions, there may be only one possibility for secure custody, but there may be an array of potential open custodial placements designated by the province.*

º You should be aware that the provincial director will rely on the predisposition report (see section 9.2.1(e) below), primarily, to decide where the young person will go to serve his or her time.

º If placement is at all an issue for your client, make yourself available to the provincial director's office and be very clear why you are trying to affect classification for the purposes of the placement. *The provincial director may be influenced in his or her decision by additional information which could be supplied by you.*

º In most places, the probation office stands in the shoes of the provincial director for this purpose.

(e) Predisposition Reports

(i) General

º A predisposition report (PDR) is a prerequisite which must be met before a custodial disposition can be made by a court: section 24(2). *It is the most important one: if there is no report, there is no custody.* The exception to this is where the requirement is waived by the Crown and the young person.

(ii) Waiver of the Predisposition Report

º You will have to decide whether it is in your client's interests to waive a PDR. You might consider consenting to a waiver in the following situations:

○ Where yourself and the Crown are making a joint submission for custody. *This is the most common reason for a waiver.*

○ Where the investigation done of your client produces a PDR that would be disastrous to your position. *There are times when it is better for you to control the presentation of damaging information.*

○ Where your client has a lengthy record, and is being held in a detention centre (temporary facility, often a jail with a "youth wing" or "youth cells"), as opposed to a youth centre (permanent youth facility) you may wish to waive a PDR and rely on an update from the detention centre or your own assessor. An immediate resolution will result in your client being sent to a youth centre which generally has more suitable programming and which your client may prefer. Unfortunately, section 7(1) of the *Act* seems to preclude the use of a youth centre pending disposition. You may however; be able to negotiate a stay in a youth centre pending disposition with the superintendent at the facility (a "provincial director") and thus alleviate the need for immediate resolution and the waiving of a PDR.

○ You should almost *never* suggest a PDR be prepared on a case simply so that a person with more time or better information-gathering abilities can do the work. *The reason for this basic rule is clear: once there is a PDR in front of the court, a custodial disposition becomes a clear possibility. Second, what you do not know can hurt you.* See a study done by Deborah K. Hanscom in 1988: *The Dynamics of Disposition in Youth Court: A report on a Survey of Youth Court Judges on Matters Affecting Disposition. This study reveals that reliance on the PDR can be dangerous. The PDR cannot be seen as a neutral fact gathering document and can be potentially harmful to the defence.*

A PDR may be submitted orally, with leave of the court. In some jurisdictions, there is a procedure called a ''stand-down'' PDR, where the case is stood down so that a probation officer can interview the client and his or her parents to make a short, verbal report to the court for the purposes of the dispositional hearing. These types of PDRs are more common in areas where duty counsel acts as counsel on first appearance pleas. Where the PDR is oral, the court must consider whether all the components of section 14 of the *Young Offenders Act* are present. Courts of Appeal have sent matters back for reconsideration where the appellate court is unsatisfied with the quality of the PDR: *R. v. H. (M.A.)* (1988), 5 W.C.B. (2d) 192 (B.C. Co. Ct.); *R. v. I. (R.)* (1985), 17 C.C.C. (3d) 523 (Ont. C.A.); *R. v. B. (J.D.)*, [1987] B.C.W.L.D. 1008, [1987] W.D.F.L. 665 (C.A.).

9.2.2 NON-CUSTODIAL DISPOSITIONS

- ° The disposing court has the following options under section 20 of the *Young Offenders Act*:

  - ° Absolute discharge, where it is in the offender's best interests and not contrary to the public interest.

  - ° Conditional discharge

  - ° Occasionally, you might find it possible to arrange a joint submission with the Crown attorney for absolute discharge if certain restitution or amends are made during a remand period (an informal "conditional discharge").

  - ° A fine, not exceeding $1,000, with terms fixed by the court.

    - ° The court is bound by section 21 of the *Young Offenders Act* to examine the present and future means of the young person before ordering a fine.

    - ° Some provinces have officially designated 'fine option programs' wherein a young person can earn credits to discharge the fine by performing work in a program designated for the purpose. The court is bound to consider whether or not the young person is a suitable candidate for such an order.

  - ° Order restitution for loss or damage to property, or compensation for personal injury

    - ° Note, restitution can be ordered only where the value of the loss is readily ascertainable.

o Note, also, no maximum limit is set under the section, but the section cannot be used to order general damages.

o Order restitution in kind or through personal service.

o Order a community service to be performed.

o Technically, the court is not to order the services unless the provincial director has a program in place or the court is satisfied that the person or organization for whom the service is to be performed has agreed to its performance. *In many jurisidictions, such proof is rarely demonstrated to the court (the service is simply set in number of hours).*

o Where the provincial director has reduced the number of options available to the court by declining to recruit (or is unable to recruit) a community organization to take young person on community service orders, a challenge to the province's ability to do so might be considered. You may be able to find a willing agency and present this option to the court.

o Under no circumstances shall the service order be for more than 240 hours, or take longer than 12 months to complete.

o A young person may later apply for an extension of time.

o Make any order of prohibition, seizure or forfeiture available under any Act of Parliament.

o Place the young person on probation for a period not exceeding two years.

o The power to order terms and conditions is very wide. *The complete list of available conditions are set out in section 23 of the Young Offenders Act and are concluded with a catch-all of "such other reasonable con-*

ditions . . ." Practices will vary from jurisdiction to jurisdiction.

○ Know local practices before suggesting treatment or counselling and seek your client's consent to attendance for treatment, where appropriate. *Some youth court judges will use the probation order to ensure attendance for treatment or counselling as directed by the probation officer. This seems to fly in the face of provincial consent-to-treatment legislation and is, therefore, not employed by all youth court judges. Keep in mind that the youth court has no power to order a youth into treatment as a disposition per se.*

○ Note, too, the power of the court to order the young person to reside where placed by the provincial director.

○ The unavailability of certain non-custodial options in some jurisdictions is not grounds for *Charter* relief: *R. v. S. (S.)*, [1990] 2 S.C.R. 254, 77 C.R. (3d) 273, 57 C.C.C. (3d) 115; *R. v. S. (G.)*, [1990] 2 S.C.R. 294, 77 C.R. (3d) 303, 57 C.C.C. (3d) 92.

○ Order the young person into custody as discussed above.

○ Impose other reasonable and ancillary conditions as advisable in the best interests of the young person and the public.

9.3 SUBMISSIONS ON DISPOSITION

9.3.1 THE PRINCIPLES UNDERLYING THE *ACT*

In addition to the traditional considerations which inform the sentencing process in adult matters, there are additional policies enshrined in section 3 of the *Young Offenders Act* which must be applied by a court in the case of young persons.

○ Never underestimate the power of an argument which pleads one of the principles set out in section 3.

○ Section 3 should be seen as embracing a list of potential mitigating considerations, particular to young persons, which supplement the already benign sentencing scheme of the legislation.

○ Of particular importance are the following:

  ○ A multi-disciplinary approach to crime prevention is favoured: section 3(1)(a).

  ○ Bearing responsibility is not synonymous with suffering adult-like accountability: section 3(1)(a.1).

  ○ The antecedents to the criminal behaviour are relevant, as reasonable measures should be taken by society to prevent criminal behaviour in teens: section 3(1)(*b*).

  ○ Rehabilitation through addressing the needs of the youth is the best means of achieving the protection of society: section 3(1)(c.1).

  ○ Young persons are entitled to the least possible interference with freedom that is consistent with protection of society: section 3(1)(*f*).

  ○ Young persons should only be removed from their families when measures cannot be taken which would provide for continuing parenting: section 3(1)(*h*).

○ Always canvass these principles and determine whether they are factors the court should be considering in a particular case.

9.3.2 INFORMATION ABOUT CLIENT'S SITUATION

○ Always know something about the sentencing philosophy of the judge sitting on disposition.

  ○ You can then target and call evidence on facts that may be important to the particular jurist, but absent from the

75

PDR. *For example, some judges like to know how a young person does in pre-trial detention. Often the probation officer who has prepared the PDR has not approached anyone from the unit to interview, or may have relied totally on the "incident report" log from the particular setting. In Ontario, ministry policy specifically allows special reports from front line workers when specially requested by defense counsel.*

○ Tell the court about your client. *Judges like and need information before they can dispose of a case. Although the severity of the offence will be a guiding factor, a complete picture of your client can help the court if there is to be an element of planning done in the disposition.*

   ○ You will need all of the information which you collected on the first interview.

   ○ At a minimum, inform the court of the following:

      ○ age and domestic situation of your client (living at home; number of siblings etc.);

      ○ academic update;

      ○ the success of your client on any previous disposition;

      ○ support systems which exist in the community for your client (parents, youth services);

      ○ demonstrated strengths of your client in the community;

      ○ any remorse for the offence articulated or demonstrated by your client.

○ Obtain a copy of the PDR prior to the day of the disposition hearing, if possible. *Many probation offices try to have the report to the court two days before the hearing.*

○ Consider contacting the probation officer assigned to write the PDR.

○ Some probation officers will speak to defence counsel and give you some idea about the contents of the report, some will not.

○ Occasionally, it is helpful to bring to the probation officer's attention things that he or she may not otherwise ask about when conducting interviews.

○ There may also be some areas of concern about which you can offer some clarification.

○ Have a non-custodial "plan" to present to the court. *This may serve your client well. Hanscom's study (cited above at 9.2.1(e)) also indicated that two-thirds of the responding judges considered that information regarding community alternatives was important when they were considering custodial dispositions. Such considerations are now mandated under section 24(1.1), prior to a custodial disposition.*

○ You could, for example, canvass the possibility of voluntary service at some community program whose work could be seen as 'related' to the offence.

○ Be very careful about contacting the victim of an offence. You do not want to put yourself in the position of appearing to obstruct justice by contacting a victim for resolution of a matter before a plea has been entered.

○ If the victim is to be part of a community option which you are preparing, approach the officer on the case or the probation department with the request to contact the victim.

○ If child welfare involvement is warranted, have a plan and contact person in place. Be sure to remind the court that the criminal justice system and in particular, custody, are not legitimate substitutes for social concerns: section 24(1.1)(a).

10

REVIEW OF DISPOSITIONS

10.1 RIGHT TO REVIEW

Unlike an adult sentence which cannot be varied after it has been imposed except on appeal, a young offender disposition can be reviewed by a youth court judge.

○ A review of disposition is a hearing to determine whether there is any reason to justify a change in the original order. There are several types of reviews:

  ○ An automatic review of disposition where the disposition made in respect of an offence or offences exceeds one year of custody. In such a case, the young person must be brought before the court at the end of one year for a review: sections 28(1), (2).

  ○ The situation where the youth is serving a custodial disposition, but the disposition is for less than one year. Here an application can be brought after six months from the date of the most recent disposition, or with leave of the court at any earlier time: section 28(3).

  ○ A review of a non-custodial disposition such as probation, community service, or a fine. An application for a review can be made at any time after six months from the date of the disposition, or with leave of the court, at any earlier time: section 32.

○ Advise your client at the beginning of the sentence of the review provisions. It may encourage him or her to do well in custody if there is a chance later to have the sentence varied or reduced by the court.

○ In theory, there are no limits to the number of applications of review of disposition that a party can bring. For example, you should encouarge a young person who successfully brings an application to vary the remnant of a secure custody disposition to that of open custody, to bring an application to vary his or her open custody disposition to that of probation.

○ You are not, however, obliged to continually bring applications for review if a young person has continued to perform poorly in custody.

10.2   INITIATING THE REVIEW

○ An application for a review of disposition is often initiated by the facility in which the client is serving the sentence.

○ When your client instructs you to prepare and file (in other words, *initiate*) a review, you should be aware of the following procedural rules:

    ○ A review of disposition will not be allowed where an appeal is pending: section 28(5).

    ○ Notice of the review must be given to the young person, his or her parents, and the Attorney General.

    ○ Notice should be given in advance to the provincial director, or more specifically to the secure or open custody facility where the client resides, or his or her probation officer, in order for those parties to begin preparing the progress report.

    ○ Notice must be given as directed by the rules of the youth court, or, in the absence of such direction, notice of at least five clear days must be given.

    ○ Notice may be waived or dispensed with.

    ○ For the Form of Notice required, see *Appendix B, Forms 7 and 8*.

10.3 GROUNDS FOR REVIEW

10.3.1 UNDER SECTIONS 28(3) and (4)

○ Under sections 28(3) and (4), a custodial disposition can be reviewed (other than through the mandatory one year review) where:

  ○ there has been sufficient progress made to justify a change in disposition;

  ○ the circumstances that led to the committal to custody have changed materially;

  ○ there are new services or programs now available that were not available at the time of the disposition; or

  ○ there are any other grounds the court considers appropriate. You may wish to look at the quality of the custodial time being served and determine whether or not reasons of safety or poor programming warrant a review.

○ Note, review of a disposition does not mean that the original disposition was excessive or too harsh. The *Act* clearly recognizes the ability of the individual to learn from his or her mistakes and receive benefit for the change. *Often, Crown counsel will argue that the original sentence was appropriate and should not be varied. A young person is entitled by the Act to be "rewarded" for hard work, consistent progress, and efforts to reform while serving a sentence: R. v. T. (M.) (1995), 26 W.C.B. (2d) 488 (Y. Terr. Ct.).*

10.3.2 UNDER SECTION 32(2)

○ Under section 32(2), a non-custodial disposition can be reviewed where:

  ○ there has been a material change in circumstances;

° the young person is unable to comply with or is experiencing serious difficulty in complying with the terms of the disposition;

° the terms of the disposition are adversely affecting the opportunities available to the young person to obtain services, education or employment; or

° other grounds exist that the court considers appropriate.

10.4 JURISDICTION

° It is generally considered necessary for you to attempt to review each sentence individually before the original sentencing judge. Jurisprudence suggests that the review of disposition should be brought before the same judge who ordered the original disposition (see: *R. v. S.W.P.O.* (1988), 5 W.C.B. (2d) 130 (Ont. Prov. Div.). However, the review sections only refer to a review being heard before a "youth court judge". Thus, arguably any youth court judge has the power to vary his or her own or another youth court judge's order.

° Where the client is living in a jurisdiction *other* than the one where the offence occurred, consider which jurisdiction is more likely to grant your client's application for review, and bring the application there.

10.5 THE PROGRESS REPORT

° The progress report is mandatory and is a very influential and persuasive document which is prepared by the institution or youth worker and which is before the court on a review. With leave of the court, the report can be made orally.

° Find out who is preparing the report and contact that person.

° Clarify or have your client address areas with which the writer has particular concern.

- Provide any additional information which may benefit your client to the author of the report.

- You may wish to arrange a "case conference" at the facility with you, your client and the professionals involved in the plan of care as well as any outside resources.

- Any recommendation made by the progress report will be seriously considered by the court.

  - If the contact you have with the institution strongly suggests that the report will not be supporting a change in disposition at this time, discuss with the client the possibility of adjourning the application to improve his or her chances for a successful review (see *Appendix B, Form 1* for the form for a Notice of Motion for Adjournment).

  - If the client agrees and if during the intervening time his or her attitude and behavior improves, emphasize the insight and change on the return date of the review.

10.6 EVIDENCE AND SUBMISSIONS AT A REVIEW HEARING

- If the plan is to have your client return home, should the review be successful, make sure the client's parents or family is present in the court.

  - Have the parents testify at the review hearing, if necessary or helpful.

- General deterrence was a factor which lead to the client's original disposition (see *R. v. M. (J.J.)*, [1993] 2 S.C.R. 421, 20 C.R. (4th) 295, 81 C.C.C. (3d) 487), therefore apply the corollary of the principle on a dispositional review. Your argument will run along these lines:

  - The client is performing well in custody, is being compliant with the program and has a minimal number of "incident reports". The court should consider the message sent back to the other young offenders in the facility, if this particular client is denied any relief on review. Where is the incentive for participation in program and hard work if reward is unlikely?

○ Remind the court where appropriate about the sentencing principles underlying the *Young Offenders Act*, see section 9.3.1 above.

10.7 DISPOSITIONS AVAILABLE

○ The available dispositions on a review application are as follows:

  ○ The court may confirm the disposition: section 28(17)(*a*);

  ○ Where your client is in secure custody, the court may direct that he or she be placed in open custody: section 28(17)(*b*); or

  ○ The court may release your client from open or secure custody and place him or her on probation: section 28(17)(*c*);

  ○ Where your client is serving a disposition pursuant to section 20(*k*.1), the court may place your client under conditional supervision: section 28(17)(*c*).

  ○ Neither the orders of probation nor conditional supervision can exceed the remainder of the original order which was varied.

10.8 PROVINCIAL DIRECTOR'S RECOMMENDATIONS FOR CHANGE

Section 29 of the *Act* allows for a recommendation from the provincial director to transfer a young person from secure to open custody, or from open custody to probation, on notice to the young person, his or her parent and the Attorney General. If none of the parties requests a review, the court can make the order recommended. If the court deems this unadvisable, the provincial director is given an opportunity to have the disposition reviewed.

11

RECORDS

11.1 PROVISIONS GOVERNING RECORDS

○ Maintenance and destruction of records is governed by sections 40-46 of the *Young Offenders Act.*

11.2 WHAT A RECORD IS

○ Records include:

- ○ youth court files;

- ○ police records of offence, included those in the RCMP central repository;

- ○ government or private or personal records collected for the purposes of administering alternative measures, probation or other dispositions;

- ○ fingerprints or photographs collected pursuant to the *Identification of Criminals Act.*

11.3 TIME LIMITS FOR DESTRUCTION OF RECORDS

○ Records destruction for young persons is governed by section 45 of the *Act.*

- ○ Where a young person is acquitted for reasons other than a finding of not criminally responsible by reason of mental disorder, the information relating to them is to be destroyed two months after the appeal period or if appealed, three months after all proceedings in the appeal are completed.

o Records of an indictable offence must be destroyed five years after the expiration of the disposition or any intervening indictable dispositions.

o Records of a summary conviction offence must be destroyed three years after the expiry of the disposition, provided there are no new convictions.

o Records in a case where alternative measures are used are to be destroyed two years after the young person consents to participate in alternative measures (and not after the charge is withdrawn).

o Where the charge is withdrawn, the records must be destroyed one year after the withdrawal.

o Where the charge is dismissed for a reason other than acquittal [under section 19(2)], the records must be destroyed after one year.

o Where the young person receives an absolute discharge, the records are to be destroyed one year after the finding of guilt.

o Where a conditional discharge is granted, destruction of the records is to occur on the expiration of three years after the finding of guilt.

o Where the charge is stayed and no proceedings taken for one year, destruction is to occur at the end of that year. *Note that some provinces stay a charge when alternative measures is entered into.*

o The police may maintain a special records repository for serious offences. Records that would otherwise be destroyed are to be transferred to this repository: section 45 (2.1); 45(2.2); 45.02. The *Act* sets out a schedule of the offences considered serious. Refer to the back of *Appendix*

A for the schedule. Records of serious (scheduled) offences can be kept for five years or longer if the young
person is found guilty of further scheduled offences. Records relating to convictions of murder, attempt murder,
manslaughter and aggravated sexual assault can be kept
indefinitely in the repository.

○ The Royal Canadian Mounted Police may establish a repository in which to keep fingerprints and specific identifying information for up to five years from their receipt by
the repository. The prints may be disclosed for identification
purposes by the police: section 45.03.

○ A young person is deemed not to have committed any
offence when the time comes for the record to be destroyed
or transferred to the special repository: section 45(4).

○ Note that the record-keeper has discretion to destroy the
records earlier than prescribed by the *Act*: section 45(3).

11.4 LETTER REQUIRING DESTRUCTION OF RECORDS

○ You should write a letter to the chief of police or the Criminal
Records Department at the police station requiring the destruction of records upon the expiration of the time limits
found in section 11.3 above. Familiarize yourself with the
requirements of the relevant police station. For example,
some stations require that the young person sign a consent
form or that they make the request personally.

○ *Appendix B, Form 9* contains a sample of such a letter.

11.5 ACCESS TO YOUTH COURT RECORDS

○ Access to youth court records is generally prohibited. The
exceptions to publication of the identity of the young person
are discussed above in chapter 6.

° Access to records is permitted under section 44.1 to the young person, counsel, crown attorney, parent or adult assisting the youth in court or during the disposition, the court, the police, court administrators, government report writers, government administrators of alternative measures programs, government persons supervising young persons or their dispositions, persons considering parole or pardons, persons designated by regulation, and persons determining security clearance. If faced with an access request you will want to double-check the statute to ensure that access is permitted.

° You may find yourself in a situation in which another party brings an application to youth court to seek access to your client's records.

° The governing test under section 45.1 (1) of the *Act* is:

  ° whether or not the party has a valid and substantial interest in the records;

  ° whether disclosure is necessary for the proper administration of justice; and,

  ° the disclosure is not otherwise statutorily prohibited.

° Disclosure can also be ordered under section 44.1(k) to:

  ° a person or class of persons with a valid interest where desirable in the public interest for:

  ° research or statistical purposes; or

  ° for the proper administration of justice.

° An example of when access might be sought to your client's records is if your client is a complainant in another matter. You should be aware that one Ontario Youth Court Judge has held that the accused who sought access to records in such a case had no valid interest in the young person's youth court record including his criminal record and court recordings: *R. v. Mason* (March 5, 1996), (Ont. Prov. Div.) [unreported].

o Another example of when your client's records might be sought is in school disciplinary proceedings. The issue of the appropriateness of this type of access is an open-ended one and you may be in a position to exclude reference to your client's youth court matters. The disclosure of the record in this context is obviously very prejudicial to your client.

o *Note that your client does not have the power to waive his or her privacy interests as enshrined in the Y.O.A. and therefore his or her consent to the release of his or her record or identity will not excuse a violation of the Act.*

o The *Act* creates offences for breaching the publicity and disclosure provisions: sections 46 and 38(2).

12

MISCELLANEOUS

12.1 CHARTER RELIEF

○ You should always examine a youth court matter from the standpoint of the possibility of seeking relief under the *Canadian Charter of Rights and Freedoms*. In addition to the traditional grounds relied upon for adults, you will want to look to inequities in the youth system. For example, you may wish to use section 15 of the *Charter* to challenge the fact that while adults can obtain a conditional sentence, this disposition is not available under the *Young Offenders Act*. You should also be aware that section 12 of the *Charter* ("cruel and unusual punishment") was utilized to stay proceedings against youth for mischief in their holding cell, given the conditions in the cell and the overall treatment of youth by the guards: *R. v. M. (T.)* (1991), 4 O.R. (3d) 203, 7 C.R. (4th) 55 (Prov. Div.). A similar argument might be used to ask for a stay of disposition or mitigation of disposition for a youth who is faced with abuses during his or her custodial term: *MacPherson v. R.* (1996), 48 C.R. (4th) 122, (*sub nom. MacPherson v. New Brunswick*) (1996), 106 C.C.C. (3d) 271 (Q.B.) (*MacPherson* is a case involving an adult. The arguments would be even more compelling for a young person).

○ When making a Charter argument, rely on the principles in section 3 of the *Act* and refer to the special approach that is recognized with respect to young persons.

○ Check your provincial *Courts of Justice Act* or other applicable court rules or practice directions for any requirements and notice provisions for a *Notice of Constitutional Question*. A sample *Notice of Constitutional Question* can be found in *Appendix B, Form 11*.

12.2 SITUATIONS COMMON TO YOUTH IN THE CRIMINAL JUSTICE SYSTEM

° Young people are often approached by the police for invalid reasons. Consider whether or not your client was properly arrested.

° If your client is a victim of police violence, you should advise them of the local complaints procedures in your community.

° Your client will require detailed explanations of the court process and of any alternative measures options. Your client may be unable to tell you the outcome of previous charges with any accuracy.

° Your client may have problems in several aspects of his or her life. The more resources that your client is "linked up" with, the better his or her chances on disposition. With your client's permission, seek the assistance of sympathetic outside agencies, legal clinics and your provincial child advocate (see *Appendix D* for a list of advocates). This will ultimately make your job easier.

12.3 SURRENDERING A CLIENT

° Should you have a client who is at large or in custody on other charges, you may have to arrange for the surrender of your client to the police or to the court. You should attend with your client if possible and should advise your client against making statements. If your client is in custody, you will need a Judges' Order. A sample order and affidavit in support of the order are found at *Appendix B, Form 12* and *Form 13.* You should arrange with the court and local police to have the client surrender to the court to avoid his or her being detained in a detention centre. In either situation, you should be prepared to negotiate release or to conduct a bail hearing.

12.4 SECTION 26: BREACH OF DISPOSITION

° The *Young Offenders Act* has its own provision creating an offence of breach of disposition. If your client is charged with a breach, (usually a breach of probation) it is likely a breach under section 26 of the *Y.O.A.*

Appendix A

Young Offenders Act R.S.C. 1985, c. Y-1 Am. R.S. 1985, c. 27 (1st Supp.), ss. 187, 203; c. 24 (2d Supp.), ss. 1–44; c. 1 (3d Supp.), s. 12; c. 1 (4th supp.), ss. 38–45; 1991, c. 43, ss. 31–35; 1992, c. 1, s. 143; 1992, c. 11, ss. 1–13; 1992, c. 47, ss. 81–83; 1993, c. 45, s. 15, 1994, c. 26, s. 76; 1995, c. 19, ss. 1–36; 1995, c. 22, ss. 16, 17 (Sch. III, item 10), 25; 1995, c. 27, s. 2.

An Act respecting young offenders

SHORT TITLE

Short title.
1. This Act may be cited as the *Young Offenders Act.*

INTERPRETATION

Definitions — Words and expressions.
2. (1) In this Act,

"adult" means a person who is neither a young person nor a child;

"alternative measures" means measures other than judicial proceedings under this Act used to deal with a young person alleged to have committed an offence;

"child" means a person who is or, in the absence of evidence to the contrary, appears to be under the age of twelve years;

"disposition" means a disposition made under section 20 or sections 28 to 32 and includes a confirmation or a variation of a disposition;

"disposition" means a disposition made under any of sections 20, 20.1 and 28 to 32, and includes a confirmation or a variation of a disposition; 1995, c. 39, s. 177. Not in force at date of publication.

"offence" means an offence created by an Act of Parliament or by any regulation, rule, order, by-law or ordinance made thereunder other than an ordinance of the Yukon Territory or the Northwest Territories;

"offence" means an offence created by an Act of Parliament or by any regulation, rule, order, by-law or ordinance made thereunder, other than an ordinance of the Yukon Territory or the Northwest Territories or a law made by the Legislature for Nunavut or continued by section 29 of the Nunavut Act. 1993, c. 28, s. 78 (Schedule III, item 144). Not in force at date of publication.

"ordinary court" means the court that would, but for this Act, have jurisdiction in respect of an offence alleged to have been committed;

"parent" includes, in respect of another person, any person who is under a legal duty to provide for that other person or any person who has, in law or in fact, the custody or control of that other person, but does not include a person who has the custody or control of that other person by reason only of proceedings under this Act;

"predisposition report" means a report on the personal and family history and present environment of a young person made in accordance with section 14;

"progress report" means a report made in accordance with section 28 on the performance of a young person against whom a disposition has been made;

"provincial director" means a person, a group or class of persons or a body appointed or designated by or pursuant to an Act of the legislature of a province or by the Lieutenant

Governor in Council of a province or his delegate to perform in that province, either generally or in a specific case, any of the duties or functions of a provincial director under this Act;

"review board" means a review board established or designated by a province for the purposes of section 30;

"young person" means a person who is or, in the absence of evidence to the contrary, appears to be twelve years of age or more, but under eighteen years of age and, where the context requires, includes any person who is charged under this Act with having committed an offence while he was a young person or is found guilty of an offence under this Act;

"youth court" means a court established or designated by or under an Act of the legislature of a province, or designated by the Governor in Council or the Lieutenant Governor in Council of a province, as a youth court for the purposes of this Act;

"youth court judge" means a person appointed to be a judge of a youth court;

"youth worker" means a person appointed or designated, whether by title of youth worker or probation officer or by any other title, by or pursuant to an Act of the legislature of a province or by the Lieutenant Governor in Council of a province or his delegate, to perform, either generally or in a specific case, in that province any of the duties or functions of a youth worker under this Act.

(2) Unless otherwise provided, words and expressions used in this Act have the same meaning as in the *Criminal Code*. R.S. 1985, c. 24 (2nd Supp.), s. 1.

Powers, duties and functions of provincial directors.

2.1 Any power, duty or function of a provincial director under this Act may be exercised or performed by any person authorized by the provincial director to do so and, if so exercised or performed, shall be deemed to have been exercised or performed by the provincial director. R.S. 1985, c. 24 (2nd Supp.), s. 2.

DECLARATION OF PRINCIPLE

Policy for Canada with respect to young offenders — Act to be liberally construed.

3. (1) It is hereby recognized and declared that

(*a*) crime prevention is essential to the long-term protection of society and requires addressing the underlying causes of crime by young persons and developing multi-disciplinary approaches to identifying and effectively responding to children and young persons at risk of committing offending behaviour in the future;

(*a.1*) while young persons should not in all instances be held accountable in the same manner or suffer the same consequences for their behaviour as adults, young persons who commit offences should nonetheless bear responsibility for their contraventions;

(*b*) society must, although it has the responsibility to take reasonable measures to prevent criminal conduct by young persons, be afforded the necessary protection from illegal behaviour;

(*c*) young persons who commit offences require supervision, discipline and control, but, because of their state of dependency and level of development and maturity, they also have special needs and require guidance and assistance;

(*c.1*) the protection of society, which is a primary objective of the criminal law applicable to youth, is best served by rehabilitation, wherever possible, of young persons who commit offences, and rehabilitation is best achieved by addressing the needs and circumstances of a young person that are relevant to the young person's offending behaviour;

(*d*) where it is not inconsistent with the protection of society, taking no measures or taking measures other than judicial proceedings under this Act should be considered for dealing with young persons who have committed offences;

(*e*) young persons have rights and freedoms in their own right, including those stated in the *Canadian Charter of Rights and Freedoms* or in the *Canadian Bill of Rights*, and in particular a right to be heard in the course of, and to participate in, the processes that lead to decisions that affect them, and young persons should have special guarantees of their rights and freedoms;

(*f*) in the application of this Act, the rights and freedoms of young persons include a right to the least possible interference with freedom that is consistent with the protection of society, having regard to the needs of young persons and the interests of their families;

(g) young persons have the right, in every instance where they have rights or freedoms that may be affected by this Act, to be informed as to what those rights and freedoms are; and

(h) parents have responsibility for the care and supervision of their children, and, for that reason, young persons should be removed from parental supervision either partly or entirely only when measures that provide for continuing parental supervision are inappropriate.

(2) This Act shall be liberally construed to the end that young persons will be dealt with in accordance with the principles set out in subsection (1). 1995, c. 19, s. 1.

ALTERNATIVE MEASURES

Alternative measures — Restriction on use — Admissions not admissible in evidence — No bar to proceedings — Laying of information, etc.

4. (1) Alternative measures may be used to deal with a young person alleged to have committed an offence instead of judicial proceedings under this Act only if

(a) the measures are part of a program of alternative measures authorized by the Attorney General or his delegate or authorized by a person, or a person within a class of persons, designated by the Lieutenant Governor in Council of a province;

(b) the person who is considering whether to use such measures is satisfied that they would be appropriate, having regard to the needs of the young person and the interests of society;

(c) the young person, having been informed of the alternative measures, fully and freely consents to participate therein;

(d) the young person has, before consenting to participate in the alternative measures, been advised of his right to be represented by counsel and been given a reasonable opportunity to consult with counsel;

(e) the young person accepts responsibility for the act or omission that forms the basis of the offence that he is alleged to have committed;

(f) there is, in the opinion of the Attorney General or his agent, sufficient evidence to proceed with the prosecution of the offence; and

(g) the prosecution of the offence is not in any way barred at law.

(2) Alternative measures shall not be used to deal with a young person alleged to have committed an offence if the young person

(a) denies his participation or involvement in the commission of the offence; or

(b) expresses his wish to have any charge against him dealt with by the youth court.

(3) No admission, confession or statement accepting responsibility for a given act or omission made by a young person alleged to have committed an offence as a condition of his being dealt with by alternative measures shall be admissible in evidence against him in any civil or criminal proceedings.

(4) The use of alternative measures in respect of a young person alleged to have committed an offence is not a bar to proceedings against him under this Act, but

(a) where the youth court is satisfied on a balance of probabilities that the young person has totally complied with the terms and conditions of the alternative measures, the youth court shall dismiss any charge against him; and

(b) where the youth court is satisfied on a balance of probabilities that the young person has partially complied with the terms and conditions of the alternative measures, the youth court may dismiss any charge against him if, in the opinion of the court, the prosecution of the charge would, having regard to the circumstances, be unfair, and the youth court may consider the young person's performance with respect to the alternative measures before making a disposition under this Act.

(5) Subject to subsection (4), nothing in this section shall be construed to prevent any person from laying an information, obtaining the issue or confirmation of any process or proceeding with the prosecution of any offence in accordance with law.

JURISDICTION

Exclusive jurisdiction of youth court — Period of limitation — Proceedings continued when adult — Powers of youth court judge — Court of record.

5. (1) Notwithstanding any other Act of Parliament but subject to the *National Defence Act* and section 16, a youth court has exclusive jurisdiction in respect of any offence alleged to have been committed by a person while he was a young person and any such person shall be dealt with as provided in this Act.

5. (1) Notwithstanding any other Act of Parliament but subject to the Contraventions Act and the National Defence Act and section 16, a youth court has exclusive jurisdiction in respect of any offence alleged to have been committed by a person while a young person and any such person shall be dealt with as provided in this Act. 1992, c. 47, s. 81. Not in force at date of publication.

(2) No proceedings in respect of an offence shall be commenced under this Act after the expiration of the time limit set out in any other Act of Parliament or any regulation made thereunder for the institution of proceedings in respect of that offence.

(3) Proceedings commenced under this Act against a young person may be continued, after he becomes an adult, in all respects as if he remained a young person.

(4) A youth court judge, for the purpose of carrying out the provisions of this Act, is a justice and a provincial court judge and has the jurisdiction and powers of a summary conviction court under the *Criminal Code*.

(5) A youth court is a court of record. R.S. 1985, c. 27 (1st Supp.), s. 203; c. 24 (2nd Supp.), s. 3.

Certain proceedings may be taken before justices.

6. Any proceeding that may be carried out before a justice under the *Criminal Code*, other than a plea, a trial or an adjudication, may be carried out before a justice in respect of an offence alleged to have been committed by a young person, and any process that may be issued by a justice under the *Criminal Code* may be issued by a justice in respect of an offence alleged to have been committed by a young person. R.S. 1985, c. 24 (2nd Supp.), s. 4.

DETENTION PRIOR TO DISPOSITION

Designated place of temporary detention — Exception — Detention separate from adults — Transfer by provincial director — Exception relating to temporary detention — Authorization of provincial authority for detention — Determination by provincial authority of place of detention.

7. (1) A young person who is

(a) arrested and detained prior to the making of a disposition in respect of the young person under section 20, or

(b) detained pursuant to a warrant issued under subsection 32(6)

shall, subject to subsection (4), be detained in a place of temporary detention designated as such by the Lieutenant Governor in Council of the appropriate province or his delegate or in a place within a class of such places so designated.

(1.1) A young person who is detained in a place of temporary detention pursuant to subsection (1) may, in the course of being transferred from that place to the court or from the court to that place, be held under the supervision and control of a peace officer.

(2) A young person referred to in subsection (1) shall be held separate and apart from any adult who is detained or held in custody unless a youth court judge or a justice is satisfied that

(a) the young person cannot, having regard to his own safety or the safety of others, be detained in a place of detention for young persons; or

(b) no place of detention for young persons is available within a reasonable distance.

(3) A young person who is detained in custody in accordance with subsection (1) may, during the period of detention, be transferred by the provincial director from one place of temporary detention to another.

(4) Subsections (1) and (2) do not apply in respect of any temporary restraint of a young person under the supervision and control of a peace officer after arrest, but a young person who is so restrained shall be transferred to a place of temporary detention referred to in subsection (1) as soon as is reasonably practicable, and in no case later than the first reasonable opportunity after the appearance of the young person before a youth court judge or a justice pursuant to section 503 of the *Criminal Code*.

(5) In any province for which the Lieutenant Governor in Council has designated a person or a group of persons whose authorization is required, either in all circumstances or in circumstances specified by the Lieutenant Governor in Council, before a young person who has been arrested may be detained in accordance with this section, no young person shall be so detained unless the authorization is obtained.

(6) In any province for which the Lieutenant Governor in Council has designated a person or a group of persons who may determine the place where a young person who has been arrested may be detained in accordance with this section, no young person may be so detained in a place other than the one so determined. R.S. 1985, c. 24 (2nd Supp.), s. 5.

Placement of young person in care of responsible person — Condition of placement — Removing young person from care — Order — Effect of arrest.

7.1 (1) Where a youth court judge or a justice is satisfied that

(*a*) a young person who has been arrested would, but for this subsection, be detained in custody,

(*b*) a responsible person is willing and able to take care of and exercise control over the young person, and

(*c*) the young person is willing to be placed in the care of that person,

the young person may be placed in the care of that person instead of being detained in custody.

(2) A young person shall not be placed in the care of a person under subsection (1) unless

(*a*) that person undertakes in writing to take care of and to be responsible for the attendance of the young person in court when required and to comply with such other conditions as the youth court judge or justice may specify; and

(*b*) the young person undertakes in writing to comply with the arrangement and to comply with such other conditions as the youth court judge or justice may specify;

(3) Where a young person has been placed in the care of a person under subsection (1) and

(*a*) that person is no longer willing or able to take care of or exercise control over the young person, or

(*b*) it is, for any other reason, no longer appropriate that the young person be placed in the care of that person,

the young person, the person in whose care the young person has been placed or any other person may, by application in writing to a youth court judge or a justice, apply for an order under subsection (4).

(4) Where a youth court judge or a justice is satisfied that a young person should not remain in the custody of the person in whose care he was placed under subsection (1), the youth court judge or justice shall

(*a*) make an order relieving the person and the young person of the obligations undertaken pursuant to subsection (2); and

(*b*) issue a warrant for the arrest of the young person.

(5) Where a young person is arrested pursuant to a warrant issued under paragraph (4)(*b*), the young person shall be taken before a youth court judge or justice forthwith and dealt with under section 515 of the *Criminal Code*. R.S. 1985, c. 24 (2nd Supp.), s. 5.

Offence and punishment.

7.2 Any person who wilfully fails to comply with section 7, or with an undertaking entered into pursuant to subsection 7.1(2), is guilty of an offence punishable on summary conviction. R.S. 1985, c. 24 (2nd Supp.), s. 5.

Application to youth court — Notice to prosecutor — Notice to young person — Waiver of notice — Application for review under section 520 or 521 of Criminal Code — Idem — Interim release by youth court judge only — Review by court of appeal.

8. (1) [Repealed, R.S. 1985, c. 24 (2nd Supp.), s. 6.]

(2) Where an order is made under section 515 of the *Criminal Code* in respect of a young person by a justice who is not a youth court judge, an application may, at any time after the order is made, be made to a youth court for the release from or detention in custody of the young person, as the case may be, and the youth court shall hear the matter as an original application.

101

(3) An application under subsection (2) for release from custody shall not be heard unless the young person has given the prosecutor at least two clear days notice in writing of the application.

(4) An application under subsection (2) for detention in custody shall not be heard unless the prosecutor has given the young person at least two clear days notice in writing of the application.

(5) The requirement for a notice under subsection (3) or (4) may be waived by the prosecutor or by the young person or his counsel, as the case may be.

(6) An application under section 520 or 521 of the *Criminal Code* for a review of an order made in respect of a young person by a youth court judge who is a judge of a superior, county or district court shall be made to a judge of the court of appeal.

(7) No application may be made under section 520 or 521 of the *Criminal Code* for a review of an order made in respect of a young person by a justice who is not a youth court judge.

(8) Where a young person against whom proceedings have been taken under this Act is charged with an offence referred to in section 522 of the *Criminal Code*, a youth court judge, but no other court, judge or justice, may release the young person from custody under that section.

(9) A decision made by a youth court judge under subsection (8) may be reviewed in accordance with section 680 of the *Criminal Code* and that section applies, with such modifications as the circumstances require, to any decision so made. R.S. 1985, c. 24 (2nd Supp.), s. 6.

NOTICES TO PARENTS

Notice to parent in case of arrest — Notice to parent in case of summons or appearance notice — Notice to relative or other adult — Notice to spouse — Notice on direction of youth court judge or justice — Contents of notice — Notice of ticket under Contraventions Act — Service of notice — Proceedings not invalid — Exception — Where a notice not served.

9. (1) Subject to subsections (3) and (4), where a young person is arrested and detained in custody pending his appearance in court, the officer in charge at the time the young person is detained shall, as soon as possible, give or cause to be given, orally or in writing, to a parent of the young person notice of the arrest stating the place of detention and the reason for the arrest.

(2) Subject to subsections (3) and (4), where a summons or an appearance notice is issued in respect of a young person, the person who issued the summons or appearance notice, or, where a young person is released on giving his promise to appear or entering into a recognizance, the officer in charge, shall, as soon as possible, give or cause to be given, in writing, to a parent of the young person notice of the summons, appearance notice, promise to appear or recognizance.

(2.1) *Notice to parent in case of ticket* — Subject to subsections (3) and (4), a person who serves a ticket under the Contraventions Act on a young person, other than a ticket served for a contravention relating to parking a vehicle, shall, as soon as possible, give or cause to be given notice in writing of the ticket to a parent of the young person. 1992, c. 47, s. 82(1). Not in force at date of publication.

(3) Where the whereabouts of the parents of a young person

(*a*) who is arrested and detained in custody,

(*b*) in respect of whom a summons or an appearance notice is issued, or

(*c*) who is released on giving his promise to appear or entering into a recognizance

(*d*) on whom a ticket is served under the Contraventions Act other than a ticket served for a contravention relating to parking a vehicle, 1992, c. 47, s. 82(2). Not in force at date of publication.

are not known or it appears that no parent is available, a notice under this section may be given to an adult relative of the young person who is known to the young person and is likely to assist him or, if no such adult relative is available, to such other adult who is known to the young person and is likely to assist him as the person giving the notice considers appropriate.

(4) Where a young person described in paragraph 3(*a*), (*b*) or (*c*) is married, a notice under this section may be given to the spouse of the young person instead of a parent.

(4) A notice under this section may be given to the spouse of a young person described in paragraph (3)(*a*), (*b*), (*c*) or (*d*) instead of to a parent. 1992, c. 47, s. 82(g). Not in force at date of publication.

(5) Where doubt exists as to the person to whom a notice under this section should be given, a youth court judge or, where a youth court judge is, having regard to the circumstances, not reasonably available, a justice may give directions as to the person to whom the notice should be given, and a notice given in accordance with those directions is sufficient notice for the purposes of this section.

(6) Any notice under this section shall, in addition to any other requirements under this section, include

(*a*) the name of the young person in respect of whom it is given;

(*b*) the charge against the young person and the time and place of appearance; and

(*b*) the charge against the young person and, except in the case of a notice of a ticket served under the Contraventions Act, the time and place of appearance; and 1992, c. 47, s. 82(4). Not in force at date of publication.

(*c*) a statement that the young person has the right to be represented by counsel.

(6.1) A notice under subsection (2.1) shall include a copy of the ticket. 1992, c. 47, s. 84(5). Not in force at date of publication.

(7) Subject to subsections (9) and (10), a notice under this section given in writing may be served personally or may be sent by mail.

(8) Subject to subsections (9) and (10), failure to give notice in accordance with this section does not affect the validity of proceedings under this Act.

(9) Failure to give notice under subsection (2) in accordance with this section in any case renders invalid any subsequent proceedings under this Act relating to the case unless

(*a*) a parent of the young person against whom proceedings are held attends court with the young person; or

(*b*) a youth court judge or a justice before whom proceedings are held against the young person

(i) adjourns the proceedings and orders that the notice be given in such manner and to such persons as the judge or justice directs, or

(ii) dispenses with the notice where the judge or justice is of the opinion that, having regard to the circumstances, the notice may be dispensed with.

(10) Where there has been a failure to give a notice under subsection (1) in accordance with this section and none of the persons to whom such notice may be given attends court with a young person, a youth court judge or a justice before whom proceedings are held against the young person may

(10) *Where notice is not served* — Where there has been a failure to give a notice under subsection (1) or (2.1) in accordance with this section and none of the persons to whom the notice may be given attends court with the young person, a youth court judge or a justice before whom proceedings are held against the young person may
1992, c. 47, s. 86(6). Not in force at date of publication.

(*a*) adjourn the proceedings and order that the notice be given in such manner and to such person as he directs; or

(*b*) dispense with the notice where, in his opinion, having regard to the circumstances, notice may be dispensed with. R.S. 1985, c. 24 (2d Supp.), s. 7(1); 1991, c. 43, ss. 31(1), (2).

(11) [Repealed, R.S. 1985, c. 24 (2nd Supp.), s. 7(2).]

Order requiring attendance of parent — Service of order — Failure to attend — Appeal — Warrant to arrest parent.

10. (1) Where a parent does not attend proceedings before a youth court in respect of a young person, the court may, if in its opinion the presence of the parent is necessary or in the best interest of the young person, by order in writing require the parent to attend at any stage of the proceedings.

(1.1) *No order in ticket proceedings* — Subsection (1) does not apply in proceedings commenced by filing a ticket under the Contraventions Act. 1992, c. 47, s. 83. Not in force at date of publication.

(2) A copy of any order made under subsection (1) shall be served by a peace officer or by a person designated by a youth court by delivering it personally to the parent to whom it is directed, unless the youth court authorizes service by registered mail.

(3) A parent who is ordered to attend a youth court pursuant to subsection (1) and who fails without reasonable excuse, the proof of which lies on that parent, to comply with the order

(*a*) is guilty of contempt of court;

(*b*) may be dealt with summarily by the court; and

(*c*) is liable to the punishment provided for in the *Criminal Code* for a summary conviction offence.

(4) Section 10 of the *Criminal Code* applies where a person is convicted of contempt of court under subsection (3).

(5) If a parent who is ordered to attend a youth court pursuant to subsection (1) does not attend at the time and place named in the order or fails to remain in attendance as required and it is proved that a copy of the order was served on the parent, a youth court may issue a warrant to compel the attendance of the parent. R.S. 1985, c. 24 (2nd Supp.), s. 8(1).

(6) [Repealed, R.S., c. 24 (2nd Supp.), s. 8(2).]

RIGHT TO COUNSEL

Right to retain counsel — Arresting officer to advise young person of right to counsel — Justice, youth court or review board to advise young person of right to counsel — Trial, hearing or review before youth court or review board — Appointment of counsel — Release hearing before justice — Young person may be assisted by adult — Counsel independent of parents — Statement of right to counsel.

11. (1) A young person has the right to retain and instruct counsel without delay, and to exercise that right personally, at any stage of proceedings against the young person and prior to and during any consideration of whether, instead of commencing or continuing judicial proceedings against the young person under this Act, to use alternative measures to deal with the young person.

(2) Every young person who is arrested or detained shall, forthwith on his arrest or detention, be advised by the arresting officer or the officer in charge, as the case may be, of his right to be represented by counsel and shall be given an opportunity to obtain counsel.

(3) Where a young person is not represented by counsel

(*a*) at a hearing at which it will be determined whether to release the young person or detain him in custody prior to disposition of his case,

(*b*) at a hearing held pursuant to section 16,

(*c*) at his trial,

(*c*.1) at any proceedings held pursuant to subsection 26.1(1), 26.2(1) or 26.6(1),

(*d*) at a review of a disposition held before a youth court or a review board under this Act, or

(*e*) at a review of the level of custody pursuant to subsection 28.1(1),

the justice before whom, or the youth court or review board before which, the hearing, trial or review is held shall advise the young person of his right to be represented by counsel and shall give the young person a reasonable opportunity to obtain counsel.

(4) Where a young person at his trial or at a hearing or review referred to in subsection (3) wishes to obtain counsel but is unable to do so, the youth court before which the hearing, trial or review is held or the review board before which the review is held

(*a*) shall, where there is a legal aid or assistance program available in the province where the hearing, trial or review is held, refer the young person to that program for the appointment of counsel; or

(*b*) where no legal aid or assistance program is available or the young person is unable to obtain counsel through such a program, may, and on the request of the young person shall, direct that the young person be represented by counsel.

(5) Where a direction is made under paragraph (4)(*b*) in respect of a young person, the Attorney General of the province in which the direction is made shall appoint counsel, or cause counsel to be appointed, to represent the young person.

(6) Where a young person at a hearing before a justice who is not a youth court judge at which it will be determined whether to release the young person or detain him in custody prior to disposition of his case wishes to obtain counsel but is unable to do so, the justice shall

(*a*) where there is a legal aid or assistance program available in the province where the hearing is held,

(i) refer the young person to that program for the appointment of counsel, or

(ii) refer the matter to a youth court to be dealt with in accordance with paragraph 4(*a*) or (*b*); or

(*b*) where no legal aid or assistance program is available or the young person is unable to obtain counsel through such a program, refer the matter to a youth court to be dealt with in accordance with paragraph (4)(*b*).

(7) Where a young person is not represented by counsel at his trial or at a hearing or review referred to in subsection (3), the justice before whom or the youth court or review board before which the proceedings are held may, on the request of the young person, allow the young person to be assisted by an adult whom the justice, court or review board considers to be suitable.

(8) In any case where it appears to a youth court judge or a justice that the interests of a young person and his parents are in conflict or that it would be in the best interest of the young person to be represented by his own counsel, the judge or justice shall ensure that the young person is represented by counsel independent of his parents.

(9) A statement that a young person has the right to be represented by counsel shall be included in

(*a*) any appearance notice or summons issued to the young person;

(*b*) any warrant to arrest the young person;

(*c*) any promise to appear given by the young person;

(*d*) any recognizance entered into before an officer in charge by the young person;

(*e*) any notice given to the young person in relation to any proceedings held pursuant to subsection 26.1(1), 26.2(1) or 26.6(1); or

(*f*) any notice of a review of a disposition given to the young person. R.S. 1985, c. 24 (2nd Supp.), s. 9; 1992, c. 11, s. 1; 1995 c. 19, s. 2.

APPEARANCE

Where young person appears — Waiver — Where young person not represented by counsel — Idem — Where youth court not satisfied — Idem.

12. (1) Where a young person against whom an information is laid must first appear before a youth court judge or a justice, and the judge or justice shall

(*a*) cause the information to be read to the young person;

(*b*) where the young person is not represented by counsel, inform the young person of the right to be so represented; and

(*c*) where the young person is a young person referred to in subsection 16(1.01), inform the young person that the young person will be proceeded against in ordinary court in accordance with the law ordinarily applicable to an adult charged with the offence unless an application is made to the youth court by the young person, the young person's counsel or the Attorney General or an agent of the Attorney General to have the young person proceeded against in the youth court and an order is made to that effect.

(2) A young person may waive the requirement under paragraph (1)(*a*) where the young person is represented by counsel.

(3) Where a young person is not represented in youth court by counsel, the youth court shall, before accepting a plea,

(*a*) satisfy itself that the young person understands the charge against him; and

(*b*) explain to the young person that he may plead guilty or not guilty to the charge.

(3.1) Where a young person is a young person referred to in subsection 16(1.01) and is not represented in youth court by counsel, the youth court shall satisfy itself that the young person understands (*a*) the charge against the young person;

(*b*) the consequences of being proceeded against in ordinary court; and(*c*) the young person's right to apply to be proceeded against in youth court.

(4) Where the youth court is not satisfied that a young person understands the charge against him, as required under paragraph (3)(*a*), the court shall enter a plea of not guilty on behalf of the young person and shall proceed with the trial in accordance with subsection 19(2).

(5) Where the youth court is not satisfied that a young person understands the matters referred to in subsection (3.1), the court shall direct that the young person be represented by counsel. 1995, c. 19, s. 3.

MEDICAL AND PSYCHOLOGICAL REPORTS

Medical or psychological assessment — Purpose of assessment — Custody for assessment — Presumption against custodial remand — Report of qualified person in writing — Application to vary assessment order where circumstances change — Custody for assessment — Disclosure of report — Cross-examination — Report to be withheld where disclosure unnecessary or prejudicial — Report to be withheld where disclosure dangerous to any person — Idem — Reports to be part of record — Disclosure by qualified person — Definition of "qualified person".

13. (1) A youth court may, at any stage of proceedings against a young person

(*a*) with the consent of the young person and the prosecutor, or

(*b*) on its own motion or on application of the young person or the prosecutor, where

(i) the court has reasonable grounds to believe that the young person may be suffering from a physical or mental illness or disorder, a psychological disorder, an emotional disturbance, a learning disability or a mental disability,

(ii) the young person's history indicates a pattern of repeated findings of guilt under this Act, or

(iii) the young person is alleged to have committed an offence involving serious personal injury, and the court believes a medical, psychological or psychiatric report in respect of the young person is necessary for a purpose mentioned in paragraphs (2)(*a*) to (*e*),

by order require that the young person be assessed by a qualified person and require the person who conducts the examination to report the results thereof in writing to the court.

(2) A youth court may make an order under subsection (1) in respect of a young person for the purpose of

(*a*) considering an application under section 16;

(*b*) making or reviewing a disposition under this Act, other than a disposition made under section 672.54 or 672.58 of the *Criminal Code*;

(*c*) considering an application under subsection 26.1(1);

(*d*) setting conditions under subsection 26.2(1); or

(*e*) making an order under subsection 26.6(2); or

(*f*) authorizing disclosure under subsection 38(1.5).

(3) Subject to subsections (3.1) and (3.3), for the purpose of an assessment under this section, a youth court may remand a young person to such custody as it directs for a period not exceeding thirty days.

(3.1) A young person shall not be remanded in custody pursuant to an order made by a youth court under subsection (1) unless

(*a*) the youth court is satisfied that on the evidence custody is necessary to conduct an assessment of the young person, or that on the evidence of a qualified person detention of the young person in custody is desirable to conduct the assessment of the young person and the young person consents to custody; or

(*b*) the young person is required to be detained in custody in respect of any other matter or by virtue of any provision of the *Criminal Code.*

(3.2) For the purposes of paragraph (3.1)(*a*), when the prosecutor and the young person agree, evidence of a qualified person may be received in the form of a report in writing.

(3.3) A youth court may, at any time while an order in respect of a young person made by the court under subsection (1) is in force, on cause being shown, vary the terms and conditions specified in that order in such manner as the court considers appropriate in the circumstances.

(4) Where a youth court receives a report made in respect of a young person pursuant to subsection (1),

    (*a*) the court shall, subject to subsection (6), cause a copy of the report to be given to

        (i) the young person,

        (ii) a parent of the young person, if the parent is in attendance at the proceedings against the young person,

        (iii) counsel, if any, representing the young person, and

        (iv) the prosecutor; and

    (*b*) the court may cause a copy of the report to be given to a parent of the young person not in attendance at the proceedings against the young person if the parent is, in the opinion of the court, taking an active interest in the proceedings.

(5) Where a report is made in respect of a young person pursuant to subsection (1), the young person, his counsel or the adult assisting him pursuant to subsection 11(7) and the prosecutor shall, subject to subsection (6), on application to the youth court, be given an opportunity to cross-examine the person who made the report.

(6) A youth court shall withhold all or part of a report made in respect of a young person pursuant to subsection (1) from a private prosecutor, where disclosure of the report or part, in the opinion of the court, is not necessary for the prosecution of the case and might be prejudicial to the young person.

(7) A youth court shall withhold all or part of a report made in respect of a young person pursuant to subsection (1) from the young person's parents or a private prosecutor where the court is satisfied, on the basis of the report or evidence given in the absence of the young person, parents or private prosecutor by the person who made the report, that disclosure of all or part of the report would seriously impair the treatment or recovery of the young person, or would be likely to endanger the life or safety of, or result in serious psychological harm to, another person.

(8) Notwithstanding subsection (7), the youth court may release all or part of the report referred to in that subsection to the young person, the young person's parents or the private prosecutor where the interests of justice make disclosure essential in the court's opinion.

(9) A report made pursuant to subsection (1) shall form part of the record of the case in respect of which it was requested.

(10) Notwithstanding any other provision of this Act, a qualified person who is of the opinion that a young person held in detention or committed to custody is likely to endanger his own life or safety or to endanger the life of, or cause bodily harm to, another person may immediately so advise any person who has the care and custody of the young person whether or not the same information is contained in a report made pursuant to subsection (1).

(11) In this section, "qualified person" means a person duly qualified by provincial law to practice medicine or psychiatry or to carry out psychological examinations or assessments, as the circumstances require, or, where no such law exists, a person who, is, in the opinion of the youth court, so qualified, and includes a person or a person within a class of persons designated by the Lieutenant Governor in Council of a province or his delegate. 1991, c. 43, ss. 32, 35(*a*); 1995, c. 19, s. 4.

(12) [Repealed, R.S. 1985, c. 24 (2nd Supp.), s. 10.]

Statements not admissible against young person — Exceptions.

13.1 (1) Subject to subsection (2), where a young person is assessed pursuant to an order made under subsection 13(1), no statement or reference to a statement made by the young person during the course and for the purposes of the assessment to the person who conducts the assessment or to anyone acting under that person's direction is admissible in evidence, without the consent of the young person, in any proceeding before a court, tribunal, body or person with jurisdiction to compel the production of evidence.

(2) A statement referred to in subsection (1) is admissible in evidence for the purposes of

    (*a*) considering an application under section 16 in respect of the young person;

    (*b*) determining whether the young person is unfit to stand trial;

(*c*) determining whether the balance of the mind of the young person was disturbed at the time of commission of the alleged offence, where the young person is a female person charged with an offence arising out of the death of her newly-born child;

(*d*) making or reviewing a disposition in respect of the young person;

(*e*) determining whether the young person was, at the time of the commission of an alleged offence, suffering from automatism or a mental disorder so as to be exempt from criminal responsibility by virtue of subsection 16(1) of the *Criminal Code*, if the accused puts his or her mental capacity for criminal intent into issue, or if the prosecutor raises the issue after verdict;

(*f*) challenging the credibility of a young person in any proceeding where the testimony of the young person is inconsistent in a material particular with a statement referred to in subsection (1) that the young person made previously;

(*g*) establishing the perjury of a young person who is charged with perjury in respect of a statement made in any proceeding.

(*h*) deciding an application for an order under subsection 26.1(1);

(*i*) setting the conditions under subsection 26.2(1);

(*j*) conducting a review under subsection 26.6(1); or

(*k*) deciding an application for a disclosure order under subsection 38(1.5). 1991, c. 43, s. 33; c. 43, s. 35(*b*); 1995, c. 19, s. 5.

APPLICATION OF PART XX.1 OF THE CRIMINAL CODE
(MENTAL DISORDER)

Sections of Criminal Code applicable — Notice and copies to counsel and parents — Proceedings not invalid — Exception — No hospital order assessments — Considerations of court or Review Board making a disposition — Cap applicable to young persons — Application to increase cap of unfit young person subject to transfer — Consideration of youth court for increase in cap — Prima facie case to be made every year — Designation of hospitals for young persons.

13.2 (1) Except to the extent that they are inconsistent with or excluded by this Act, section 16 and Part XX.1 of the *Criminal Code*, except sections 672.65 and 672.66, apply, with such modifications as the circumstances require, in respect of proceedings under this Act in relation to offences alleged to have been committed by young persons.

(2) For the purposes of subsection (1), wherever in Part XX.1 of the *Criminal Code* a reference is made to

(*a*) a copy to be sent or otherwise given to an accused or a party to the proceedings, the reference shall be read as including a reference to a copy to be sent or otherwise given to

(i) counsel, if any, representing the young person,

(ii) any parent of the young person who is in attendance at the proceedings against the young person, and

(iii) any parent of the young person who is, in the opinion of the youth court or Review Board, taking an active interest in the proceedings; and

(*b*) notice to be given to an accused or a party to proceedings, the reference shall be read as including a reference to notice to be given to counsel, if any, representing the young person and the parents of the young person.

(3) Subject to subsection (4), failure to give a notice referred to in paragraph (2)(*b*) to a parent of a young person does not affect the validity of proceedings under this Act.

(4) Failure to give a notice referred to in paragraph (2)(*b*) to a parent of a young person in any case renders invalid any subsequent proceedings under this Act relating to the case unless

(*a*) a parent of the young person attends at the court or Review Board with the young person; or

(*b*) a youth court judge or Review Board before whom proceedings are held against the young person

(i) adjourns the proceedings and orders that the notice be given in such manner and to such persons as the judge or Review Board directs, or

(ii) dispenses with the notice where the youth court or Review Board is of the opinion that, having regard to the circumstances, the notice may be dispensed with.

(5) A youth court may not make an order under subsection 672.11 of the *Criminal Code* in respect of a young person for the purpose of assisting in the determination of an issue mentioned in paragraph 672.11(*e*) of that Act.

(6) Before making or reviewing a disposition in respect of a young person under Part XX.1 of the *Criminal Code*, a youth court or Review Board shall consider the age and special needs of the young person and any representations or submissions made by the young person's parents.

(7) Subject to subsection (9), for the purpose of applying subsection 672.64(3) of the *Criminal Code* to proceedings under this Act in relation to an offence alleged to have been committed by a young person, the applicable cap shall be the maximum period during which the young person would be subject to a disposition by the youth court if found guilty of the offence.

(8) Where an application is made under section 16 to proceed against a young person in ordinary court and the young person is found unfit to stand trial, the Attorney General or the agent of the Attorney General may, before the youth court makes or refuses to make an order under that section, apply to the court to increase the cap that shall apply to the young person.

(9) The youth court, after giving the Attorney General and the counsel and parents of the young person in respect of whom an application is made under subsection (8) an opportunity to be heard, shall take into consideration

(*a*) the seriousness of the alleged offence and the circumstances in which it was allegedly committed,

(*b*) the age, maturity, character and background of the young person and any previous findings of guilty against the young person under any Act of Parliament,

(*c*) the likelihood that the young person will cause significant harm to any person if released on expiration of the cap that applies to the young person pursuant to subsection (7), and

(*d*) the respective caps that would apply to the young person under this Act and under the *Criminal Code*,

and the youth court shall, where satisfied that the application under section 16 would likely succeed if the young person were fit to stand trial, apply to the young person the cap that would apply to an adult for the same offence.

(10) For the purpose of applying subsection 672.33(1) of the *Criminal Code* to proceedings under this Act in relation to an offence alleged to have been committed by a young person, wherever in that subsection a reference is made to two years, there shall be substituted a reference to one year.

(11) A reference in Part XX.1 of the *Criminal Code* to a hospital in a province shall be construed as a reference to a hospital designated by the Minister of Health of the province for the custody, treatment or assessment of young persons. 1991, c. 43, s. 33.

PRE-DISPOSITION REPORT

Pre-disposition report — Contents of report — Oral report with leave — Report to form part of record — Copies of pre-disposition report — Cross-examination — Report may be withheld from private prosecutor — Report disclosed to other persons — Disclosure by the provincial director — Inadmissibility of statements.

14. (1) Where a youth court deems it advisable before making a disposition under section 20 in respect of a young person who is found guilty of an offence it may, and where a youth court is required under this Act to consider a pre-disposition report before making an order or a disposition in respect of a young person it shall, require the provincial director to cause to be prepared a pre-disposition report in respect of the young person and to submit the report to the court.

(2) A pre-disposition report made in respect of a young person shall, subject to subsection (3), be in writing and shall include,

(*a*) the results of an interview with

(i) the young person

(ii) where reasonably possible, the parents of the young person and,

(iii) where appropriate and reasonably possible, members of the young person's extended family;

(*b*) the results of an interview with the victim in the case, where applicable and where reasonably possible;

(*c*) such information as is applicable to the case including, where applicable,

(i) the age, maturity, character, behaviour and attitude of the young person and his willingness to make amends,

(ii) any plans put forward by the young person to change his conduct or to participate in activities or undertake measures to improve himself,

(iii) the history of previous findings of delinquency under the *Juvenile Delinquents Act*, chapter J-3 of the Revised Statutes of Canada, 1970, or previous findings of guilt under this Act or any other Act of Parliament or any regulation made thereunder or under an Act of the legislature of a province or any regulation made thereunder or a by-law or ordinance of a municipality, the history of community or other services rendered to the young person with respect to those findings and the response of the young person to previous sentences or dispositions and to services rendered to him,

(iv) the history of alternative measures used to deal with the young person and the response of the young person thereto,

(v) the availability of community services and facilities for young persons and the willingness of the young person to avail himself of those services or facilities,

(vi) the relationship between the young person and the young person's parents and the degree of control and influence of the parents over the young person, and where appropriate and reasonably possible, the relationship between the young person and the young person's extended family and the degree of control and influence of the young person's extended family over the young person,

(vii) the school attendance and performance record and the employment record of the young person; and

(*d*) such information as the provincial director considers relevant, including any recommendation that the provincial director considers appropriate.

(3) Where a pre-disposition report cannot reasonably be committed to writing, it may, with leave of the youth court, be submitted orally in court.

(4) A pre-disposition report shall form part of the record of the case in respect of which it was requested.

(5) Where a pre-disposition report made in respect of a young person is submitted to a youth court in writing, the court

(*a*) shall, subject to subsection (7), cause a copy of the report to be given to

(i) the young person,

(ii) a parent of the young person, if the parent is in attendance at the proceedings against the young person,

(iii) counsel, if any, representing the young person, and

(iv) the prosecutor; and

(*b*) may cause a copy of the report to be given to a parent of the young person not in attendance at the proceedings against the young person if the parent is, in the opinion of the court, taking an active interest in the proceedings.

(6) Where a pre-disposition report made in respect of a young person is submitted to a youth court, the young person, his counsel or the adult assisting him pursuant to subsection 11(7) and the prosecutor shall, subject to subsection (7), on application to the youth court, be given the opportunity to cross-examine the person who made the report.

(7) Where a pre-disposition report made in respect of a young person is submitted to a youth court, the court may, where the prosecutor is a private prosecutor and disclosure of the report or any part thereof to the prosecutor might, in the opinion of the court, be prejudicial to the young person and is not, in the opinion of the court, necessary for the prosecution of the case against the young person,

(*a*) withhold the report or part thereof from the prosecutor, if the report is submitted in writing; or (*b*) exclude the prosecutor from the court during the submission of the report or part thereof, if the report is submitted orally in court.

(8) Where a pre-disposition report made in respect of a young person is submitted to a youth court, the court

 (*a*) shall, on request, cause a copy or a transcript of the report to be supplied to

  (i) any court that is dealing with matters relating to the young person, and

  (ii) any youth worker to whom the young person's case has been assigned; and

 (*b*) may, on request, cause a copy or a transcript of the report, or a part thereof, to be supplied to any person not otherwise authorized under this section to receive a copy or transcript of the report if, in the opinion of the court, the person has a valid interest in the proceedings.

(9) A provincial director who submits a pre-disposition report made in respect of a young person to a youth court may make the report, or any part thereof, available to any person in whose custody or under whose supervision the young person is placed or to any other person who is directly assisting in the care or treatment of the young person.

(10) No statement made by a young person in the course of the preparation of a pre-disposition report in respect of the young person is admissible in evidence against him in any civil or criminal proceedings except in proceedings under section 16 or 20 or sections 28 to 32. R.S. 1985, c. 24 (2nd Supp.), s. 11; 1995, c. 19, s. 6.

DISQUALIFICATION OF JUDGE

Disqualification of judge — Exception.

15. (1) Subject to subsection (2), a youth court judge who, prior to an adjudication in respect of a young person charged with an offence, examines a pre-disposition report made in respect of the young person, or hears an application under section 16 in respect of the young person, in connection with that offence shall not in any capacity conduct or continue the trial of the young person for the offence and shall transfer the case to another judge to be dealt with according to law.

(2) A youth court judge may, in the circumstances referred to in subsection (1), with the consent of the young person and the prosecutor, conduct or continue the trial of the young person if the judge is satisfied that he has not been predisposed by information contained in the pre-disposition report or by representations made in respect of the application under section 16.

TRANSFER

Transfer to ordinary court —Trial in ordinary court for certain offences — Making of application — Where application is opposed — Deeming — Time may be extended — Order — Onus — Considerations by youth court — Pre-disposition reports — Where young person on transfer status — Court to state reasons — No further applications for transfer — Effect of order — Idem — Jurisdiction of ordinary court limited — Extension of time to make application — Notice of application — Inadmissibility of statement.

16. (1) Subject to subsection (1.01), at any time after an information is laid against a young person alleged to have, after attaining the age of fourteen years, committed an indictable offence other than an offence referred to in section 553 of the *Criminal Code* but prior to adjudication, a youth court shall, on application of the young person or the young person's counsel or the Attorney General or an agent of the Attorney General, determine, in accordance with subsection (1.1), whether the young person should be proceeded against in ordinary court.

(1.01) Every young person against whom an information is laid who is alleged to have committed

 (*a*) first degree murder or second degree murder within the meaning of section 231 of the *Criminal Code*,

 (*b*) an offence under section 239 of the *Criminal Code* (attempt to commit murder),

 (*c*) an offence under section 232 or 234 of the *Criminal Code* (manslaughter), or

 (*d*) an offence under section 273 of the *Criminal Code* (aggravated sexual assault),

and who was sixteen or seventeen years of age at the time of the alleged commission of the offence shall be proceeded against in ordinary court in accordance with the law ordinarily applicable to an adult charged with the offence unless the youth court, on application by the young person, the young person's counsel or the Attorney General or an agent of the Attorney General, makes an order under subsection (1.04) or (1.05) or subparagraph (1.1)(*a*)(ii) that the young person should be proceeded against in youth court.

(1.02) An application to the youth court under subsection (1.01) must be made orally, in the presence of the other party to the proceedings, or in writing, with a notice served on the other party to the proceedings.

(1.03) Where the other party to the proceedings referred to in subsection (1.02) files a notice of opposition to the application with the youth court within twenty-one days after the making of the oral application, or the service of the notice referred to in that subsection, as the case may be, the youth court shall, in accordance with subsection (1.1), determine whether the young person should be proceeded against in youth court.

(1.04) Where the other party to the proceedings referred to in subsection (1.02) files a notice of non-opposition to the application with the youth court within the time referred to in subsection (1.03), the youth court shall order that the young person be proceeded against in youth court.

(1.05) Where the other party to the proceedings referred to in subsection (1.02) does not file a notice referred to in subsection (1.03) or (1.04) within the time referred to in subsection (1.03), the youth court shall order that the young person be proceeded against in youth court.

(1.06) The time referred to in subsections (1.03) to (1.05) may be extended by mutual agreement of the parties to the proceedings by filing a notice to that effect with the youth court.

(1.1) In making the determination referred to in subsection (1) or (1.03), the youth court, after affording both parties and the parents of the young person an opportunity to be heard, shall consider the interest of society, which includes the objectives of affording protection to the public and rehabilitation of the young person, and determine whether those objectives can be reconciled by the youth being under the jurisdiction of the youth court, and

(*a*) if the court is of the opinion that those objectives can be so reconciled, the court shall
(i) in the case of an application under subsection (1), refuse to make an order that the young person be proceeded against in ordinary court, and
(ii) in the case of an application under subsection (1.01), order that the young person be proceeded against in youth court; or

(*b*) if the court is of the opinion that those objectives cannot be so reconciled, protection of the public shall be paramount and the court shall
(i) in the case of an application under subsection (1), order that the young person be proceeded against in ordinary court in accordance with the law ordinarily applicable to an adult charged with the offence, and
(ii) in the case of an application under subsection (1.01), refuse to make an order that the young person be proceeded against in youth court.

(1.11) Where an application is made under subsection (1) or (1.01), the onus of satisfying the youth court of the matters referred to in subsection (1.1) rests with the applicant.

(2) In making the determination referred to in subsection (1) or (1.03) in respect of a young person, a youth court shall take into account

(*a*) the seriousness of the alleged offence and the circumstances in which it was allegedly committed;

(*b*) the age, maturity, character and background of the young person and any record or summary of previous findings of delinquency under the Juvenile Delinquents Act, chapter J-3 of the Revised Statutes of Canada, 1970, or previous findings of guilt under this Act or any other Act of Parliament or any regulation made thereunder;

(*c*) the adequacy of this Act, and the adequacy of the *Criminal Code* or any other Act of Parliament that would apply in respect of the young person if an order were made under this section to meet the circumstances of the case;

(*d*) the availability of treatment or correctional resources;

(*e*) any representations made to the court by or on behalf of the young person or by the Attorney General or his agent; and

(*f*) any other factors that the court considers relevant.

(3) In making the determination referred to in subsection (1) or (1.03) in respect of a young person, a youth court shall consider a pre-disposition report.

(4) Notwithstanding subsections (1) and (3), where an application is made under subsection (1) by the Attorney General or the Attorney General's agent in respect of an offence alleged to have been committed by a young person while the young person was being proceeded against in ordinary court pursuant to an order previously made under this section or serving a sentence as a result of proceedings in ordinary court, the youth court may make a further order under this section without a hearing and without considering a pre-disposition report.

(5) Where a youth court makes an order or refuses to make an order under this section, it shall state the reasons for its decision and the reasons shall form part of the record of the proceedings in the youth court.

(6) Where a youth court refuses to make an order under this section in respect of an alleged offence, no further application may be made under this section in respect of that offence.

(7) Where an order is made under this section pursuant to an application under subsection (1), proceedings under this Act shall be discontinued and the young person against whom the proceedings are taken shall be taken before the ordinary court.

(7.1) Where an order is made under this section pursuant to an application under subsection (1.01), the proceedings against the young person shall be in the youth court.

(8) Where a young person is proceeded against in ordinary court in respect of an offence by reason of

    (*a*) subsection (1.01), where no application is made under that subsection,

    (*b*) an order made under subparagraph (1.1)(*b*)(i), or

    (*c*) the refusal under subparagraph (1.1)(*b*)(ii) to make an order,

that the court has jurisdiction only in respect of that offence; or an offence included therein.

(9) An order made in respect of a young person under this section or a refusal to make such an order shall, on application of the young person or the young person's counsel or the Attorney General or the Attorney General's agent made within thirty days after the decision of the youth court, be reviewed by the court of appeal, and that court may, in its discretion, confirm or reverse the decision of the youth court.

(10) The court of appeal may, at any time, extend the time within which an application under subsection (9) may be made.

(11) A person who proposes to apply for a review under subsection (9) shall give notice of the application in such manner and within such period of time as may be directed by rules of court.

(12) No statement made by a young person in the course of a hearing held under this section is admissible in evidence against the young person in any civil or criminal proceeding held subsequent to that hearing. 1992, c. 11, s. 2; 1995, c. 19, s. 8.

(13) [Repealed 1992, c. 11, s. 16(3).]

(14) [Repealed R.S. 1985, c. 24 (2d Supp.), s. 12.]

Detention pending trial — young person under 18 — Detention pending trial — young person over 18 — Review — Who may make application — Notice — Statement of rights — Limit — age 20.

    16.1 (1) Notwithstanding anything in this or any other Act of Parliament, where a young person who is under the age of eighteen is to be proceeded against in ordinary court by reason of

    (*a*) subsection 16(1.01), where no application is made under that subsection,

    (*b*) an order under subparagraph 16(1.1)(*b*)(i), or

    (*c*) the refusal under subparagraph 16(1.1)(b)*(ii) to make an order,*

and the young person is to be in custody pending the proceedings in that court, the young person shall be held separate and apart from any adult who is detained or held in custody unless the youth court is satisfied, on application, that the young person, having regard to the best interests of the young person and the safety of others, cannot be detained in a place of detention for young persons.

(2) Notwithstanding anything in this or any other Act of Parliament, where a young person who is over the age of eighteen is to be proceeded against in ordinary court by reason of

(a) subsection 16(1.01), where no application is made under that subsection,

(b) an order under subparagraph 16(1.1)(b)(i), or

(c) the refusal under subparagraph 16(1.1)(b)(ii) to make an order,

and the young person is to be in custody pending the proceedings in that court, the young person shall be held in a place of detention for adults unless the youth court is satisfied, on application, that the young person, having regard to the best interests of the young person and the safety of others, should be detained in a place of custody for young persons.

(3) On application, the youth court shall review the placement of a young person in detention pursuant to this section and, if satisfied, having regard to the best interests of the young person and the safety of others, and after having afforded the young person, the provincial director and a representative of a provincial department responsible for adult correctional facilities an opportunity to be heard, that the young person should remain in detention where the young person is or be transferred to youth or adult detention, as the case may be, the court may so order.

(4) An application referred to in this section may be made by the young person, the young person's parents, the provincial director, the Attorney General or the Attorney General's agent.

(5) Where an application referred to in this section is made, the applicant shall cause a notice of the application to be given

(a) where the applicant is the young person or one of the young person's parents, to the provincial director and the Attorney General;

(b) where the applicant is the Attorney General or the Attorney General's agent, to the young person, the young person's parents and the provincial director; and

(c) where the applicant is the provincial director, to the young person, the parents of the young person and the Attorney General.

(6) A notice given under subsection (5) by the Attorney General or the provincial director shall include a statement that the young person has the opportunity to be heard and the right to be represented by counsel.

(7) Notwithstanding anything in this section, no young person shall remain in custody in a place of detention for young persons under this section after the young person attains the age of twenty years. 1992, c. 11, s. 2(3); 1995, c. 19, s. 9.

Placement on conviction by ordinary court — Factors to be taken into account — Report necessary — Review — Who may make application — Notice.

16.2 (1) Notwithstanding anything in this or any other Act of Parliament, where a young person who is proceeded against in ordinary court by reason of subsection 16(1.01), where no application is made under that subsection, or by reason of an order under subparagraph 16(1.1)(b)(i) or the refusal under subparagraph 16(1.1)(b)(ii) to make an order, is convicted and sentenced to imprisonment, the court shall, after affording the young person, the parents of the young person, the Attorney General, the provincial director and representatives of the provincial and federal correctional systems an opportunity to be heard, order that the young person serve any portion of the imprisonment in

(a) a place of custody for young persons separate and apart from any adult who is detained or held in custody;

(b) a provincial correctional facility for adults; or

(c) where the sentence is for two years or more, a penitentiary.

(2) In making an order under subsection (1), the court shall take into account

(a) the safety of the young person;

(b) the safety of the public;

(c) the young person's accessibility to family;

(d) the safety of other young persons if the young person were to be held in custody in a place of custody for young persons;

(e) whether the young person would have a detrimental influence on other young persons if the young person were to be held in custody in a place of custody for young persons;

(f) the young person's level of maturity;

(*g*) the availability and suitability of treatment, educational and other resources that would be provided to the young person in a place of custody for young persons and in a place of custody for adults;

(*h*) the young person's prior experiences and behaviour while in detention or custody;

(*i*) the recommendations of the provincial director and representatives of the provincial and federal correctional facilities; and

(*j*) any other factor the court considers relevant.

(3) Prior to making an order under subsection (1), the court shall require that a report be prepared for the purpose of assisting the court.

(4) On application, the court shall review the placement of a young person in detention pursuant to this section and, if satisfied that the circumstances that resulted in the initial order have changed materially, and after having afforded the young person, the provincial director and the representatives of the provincial and federal correctional systems an opportunity to be heard, the court may order that the young person be placed in

(*a*) a place of custody for young person separate and apart from any adult who is detained or held in custody;

(*b*) a provincial correctional facility for adults, or

(*c*) where the sentence is for two years or more, a penitentiary.

(5) An application referred to in this section may be made by the young person, the young person's parents, the provincial director, a representative of the provincial and federal correctional systems and the Attorney General.

(6) Where an application referred to in this section is made, the applicant shall cause a notice of the application to be given

(*a*) Where the applicant is the young person or one of the young person's parents, to the provincial director, to representatives of the provincial and federal correction systems and to the Attorney General;

(*b*) where the applicant is the Attorney General or the Attorney General's agent, to the young person, the young person's parents and the provincial director and representatives of the provincial and federal correction systems; and

(*c*) where an applicant is the provincial director, to the young person, the parents of the young person, the Attorney General and representatives of the provincial and federal correction systems. 1992, c. 11, s. 2(3); 1995, c. 19, s. 10.

Order restricting publication of information presented at transfer hearing — Offence — Definition of "newspaper".

17. (1) Where a youth court hears an application for a transfer under section 16, it shall

(*a*) where the young person is not represented by counsel, or

(*b*) on application made by or on behalf of the young person or the prosecutor, where the young person is represented by counsel,

make an order directing that any information respecting the offence presented at the hearing shall not be published in any newspaper or broadcast before such time as

(*c*) an order for a transfer is refused or set aside on review and the time for all reviews against the decision has expired or all proceedings in respect of any such review have been completed; or

(*d*) the trial is ended, if the case is transferred to ordinary court.

(2) Every one who fails to comply with an order made pursuant to subsection (1) is guilty of an offence punishable on summary conviction.

(3) In this section, "newspaper" has the meaning set out in section 297 of the *Criminal Code.* 1995, c. 19, s. 11.

TRANSFER OF JURISDICTION

Transfer of jurisdiction.

18. Notwithstanding subsections 478(1) and (3) of the *Criminal Code*, where a young person is charged with an offence that is alleged to have been committed in one province, he may, if the Attorney General of the province where the offence is alleged to have been committed consents, appear before a youth court of any other province and,

(*a*) where the young person signifies his consent to plead guilty and pleads guilty to that offence, the court shall, if it is satisfied that the facts support the charge, find the young person guilty of the offence alleged in the information; and (*b*) where the young person does not signify his consent to plead guilty and does not plead guilty, or where the court is not satisfied that the facts support the charge, the young person shall, if he was detained in custody prior to his appearance, be returned to custody and dealt with according to law.

ADJUDICATION

Where young person pleads guilty — Where young person pleads not guilty — Application for transfer to ordinary court — Election — offence of murder — Where no election made — Preliminary inquiry — Preliminary inquiry provisions of Criminal Code — Parts XIX and XX of the Criminal Code.

19. (1) Where a young person pleads guilty to an offence charged against him and the youth court is satisfied that the facts support the charge, the court shall find the young person guilty of the offence.

(2) Where a young person charged with an offence pleads not guilty to the offence or pleads guilty but the youth court is not satisfied that the facts support the charge, the court shall, subject to subsection (4), proceed with the trial and shall, after considering the matter, find the young person guilty or not guilty or make an order dismissing the charge, as the case may be.

(3) The court shall not make a finding under this section in respect of a young person in respect of whom an application may be made under section 16 for an order that the young person be proceeded against in ordinary court unless it has inquired as to whether any of the parties to the proceedings wishes to make such an application, and, if any party so wishes, has given that party an opportunity to do so.

(4) Notwithstanding section 5, where a young person is charged with having committed first degree murder or second degree murder within the meaning of section 231 of the *Criminal Code*, the youth court, before proceeding with the trial, shall ask the young person to elect to be tried by a youth court judge alone or by a judge of a superior court of criminal jurisdiction with a jury, and where a young person elects to be tried by a judge of a superior court of criminal jurisdiction with a jury, the young person shall be dealt with as provided in this Act.

(5) Notwithstanding section 5, where an election is not made under subsection (4), the young person shall be deemed to have elected to be tried by a judge of a superior court of criminal jurisdiction with a jury and dealt with as provided for in this Act.

(5.1) Where a young person elects or is deemed to have elected to be tried by a judge of a superior court of criminal jurisdiction with a jury, the youth court shall conduct a preliminary inquiry and if, on its conclusion, the young person is ordered to stand trial, the proceedings shall be before a judge of the superior court of criminal jurisdiction with a jury.

(5.2) A preliminary inquiry referred to in subsection (5.1) shall be conducted in accordance with the provisions of Part XVIII of the *Criminal Code*, except to the extent that they are inconsistent with this Act.

(6) Proceedings under this Act before a judge of a superior court of criminal jurisdiction with a jury shall be conducted, with such modifications as the circumstances require, in accordance with the provisions of Parts XIX and XX of the *Criminal Code*, except that

(*a*) the provisions of this Act respecting the protection of privacy and young persons prevail over the provisions of the *Criminal Code*; and

(*b*) the young person is entitled to be represented in court by counsel if the young person is removed from court pursuant to subsection 650(2) of the *Criminal Code*. R.S. 1985, c. 24 (2d Supp.), s. 13; 1995, c. 19, s. 12.

DISPOSITIONS

Dispositions that may be made — Coming into force of disposition — Duration of disposition — Combined duration of dispositions — Duration of dispositions made at different times — Custody first — Conditional supervision suspended — Disposition continues when adult — Reasons for the disposition — Limitation on punishment — Application of Part XXIII of Criminal Code — Section 787 of Criminal Code does not apply — Contents of probation order — No order under section 161 of Criminal Code.

20. (1) Where a youth court finds a young person guilty of an offence, it shall consider any pre-disposition report required by the court, any representations made by the parties to the proceedings or their counsel or agents and by the parents of the young person and any other relevant information before the court, and the court shall then make any one of the following dispositions, other than the disposition referred to in paragraph (*k*.1), or any number thereof that are not inconsistent with each other, and where the offence is first degree murder or second degree murder within the meaning of section 231 of the *Criminal Code*, the court shall make the disposition referred to in paragraph (*k*.1) and may make such other disposition as the court considers appropriate:

(*a*) by order direct that the young person be discharged absolutely, if the court considers it to be in the best interests of the young person and not contrary to the public interest;

(*a*.1) by order direct that the young person be discharged on such conditions as the court considers appropriate;

(*b*) impose on the young person a fine not exceeding one thousand dollars to be paid at such time and on such terms as the court may fix;

(*c*) order the young person to pay to any other person at such time and on such terms as the court may fix an amount by way of compensation for loss of or damage to property, for loss of income or support or for special damages for personal injury arising from the commission of the offence where the value thereof is readily ascertainable, but no order shall be made for general damages;

(*d*) order the young person to make restitution to any other person of any property obtained by the young person as a result of the commission of the offence within such time as the court may fix, if the property is owned by that other person or was, at the time of the offence, in his lawful possession;

(*e*) if any property obtained as a result of the commission of the offence has been sold to an innocent purchaser, where restitution of the property to its owner or any other person has been made or ordered, order the young person to pay the purchaser, at such time and on such terms as the court may fix, an amount not exceeding the amount paid by the purchaser for the property;

(*f*) subject to section 21, order the young person to compensate any person in kind or by way of personal services at such time and on such terms as the court may fix for any loss, damage or injury suffered by that person in respect of which an order may be made under paragraph (*c*) or (*e*);

(*g*) subject to section 21, order the young person to perform a community service at such time and on such terms as the court may fix;

(*h*) make any order of prohibition, seizure or forfeiture that may be imposed under any Act of Parliament or any regulation made thereunder where an accused is found guilty or convicted of that offence;

(*h*) subject to section 20.1, make any order of prohibition, seizure or forfeiture that may be imposed under any Act of Parliament or any regulation made thereunder where an accused is found guilty or convicted of that offence; 1995, c. 39, s. 178. Not in force at date of publication.

(*i*) [Repealed 1995, c. 19, s. 13(2)].

(*j*) place the young person on probation in accordance with section 23 for a specified period not exceeding two years;

(*k*) subject to sections 24 to 24.5, commit the young person to custody, to be served continuously or intermittently, for a specified period not exceeding

(i) two years from the date of committal, or

(ii) where the young person is found guilty of an offence for which the punishment provided by the *Criminal Code* or any other Act of Parliament is imprisonment for life, three years from the date of committal;

(*k*.1) order the young person to serve a disposition not to exceed

(i) in the case of first degree murder, ten years comprised of

(A) a committal to custody, to be served continuously, for a period that shall not, subject to subsection 26.1(1), exceed four years from the date of committal, and

(B) a placement under conditional supervision to be served in the community in accordance with section 26.2; and

(*l*) impose on the young person such other reasonable and ancillary conditions as it deems advisable and in the best interest of the young person and the public.

(2) A disposition made under this section shall come into force on the date on which it is made or on such later date as the youth court specifies therein.

(3) No disposition made under this section, other than an order made under paragraph (1)(*h*), (*k*) or (*k.*1), shall continue in force for more than two years and, where the youth court makes more than one disposition at the same time in respect of the same offence, the combined duration of the dispositions, except in respect of an order made under paragraph (1)(*h*), (*k*) or (*k.*1), shall not exceed two years.

(4) Subject to subsection (4.1), where more than one disposition is made under this section in respect of a young person with respect to different offences, the continuous combined duration of those dispositions shall not exceed three years, except where one of those offences is first degree murder or second degree murder within the meaning of section 231 of the *Criminal Code*, in which case the continuous combined duration of those dispositions shall not exceed ten years in the case of first degree murder, or seven years in the case of second degree murder.

(4.1) Where a disposition is made under this section in respect of an offence committed by a young person after the commencement of, but before the completion of, any dispositions made in respect of previous offences committed by the young person,

(*a*) the duration of the disposition made in respect of the subsequent offence shall be determined in accordance with subsections (3) and (4);

(*b*) the disposition may be served consecutively to the dispositions made in respect of the previous offences; and

(*c*) the combined duration of all the dispositions may exceed three years, except where the offence is, or one of the previous offences was,

(i) first degree murder within the meaning of section 231 of the *Criminal Code*, in which case the continuous combined duration of the dispositions may exceed ten years, or

(ii) second degree murder within the meaning of section 231 of the *Criminal Code*, in which case the continuous combined duration of the dispositions may exceed seven years.

(4.2) Subject to subsection (4.3), where a young person who is serving a disposition made under paragraph (1)(*k.*1) is ordered to custody in respect of an offence committed after the commencement of, but before the completion of, that disposition, the custody in respect of that subsequent offence shall be served before the young person is placed under conditional supervision.

(4.3) Where a young person referred to in subsection (4.2) is under conditional supervision at the time the young person is ordered to custody in respect of a subsequent offence, the conditional supervision shall be suspended until the young person is released from custody.

(5) Subject to section 743.5 of the *Criminal Code*, a disposition made under this section shall continue in effect in accordance with the terms thereof, after the young person against whom it is made becomes an adult.

(6) Where a youth court makes a disposition under this section, it shall state its reasons therefor in the record of the case and shall

(*a*) provide or cause to be provided a copy of the disposition, and

(*b*) on request, provide or cause to be provided a transcript or copy of the reasons for the disposition

to the young person in respect of whom the disposition was made, the young person's counsel and parents, the provincial director, where the provincial director has an interest in the disposition, the prosecutor and, in the case of a custodial disposition made under paragraph (1)(*k*) or (*k.*1), the review board, if a review board has been established or designated.

(7) No disposition shall be made in respect of a young person under this section that results in a punishment that is greater than the maximum punishment that would be applicable to an adult who has committed the same offence.

(8) Part XXIII of the *Criminal Code* does not apply in respect to proceedings under this Act except for section 722, subsection 730(2) and sections 748, 748.1 and 749, which provisions apply with such modifications as the circumstances require.

(9) Section 787 of the *Criminal Code* does not apply in respect of proceedings under this Act.

(10) The youth court shall specify in any probation order made under paragraph (1)(*j*) the period for which it is to remain in force.

(11) Notwithstanding paragraph (1)(*h*), a youth court shall not make an order of prohibition under section 161 of the Criminal Code against a young person. R.S. 1985, c. 27 (1st Supp.), s. 187, Schedule; c. 24 (2d Supp.), s. 14; c. 1 (4th Supp.), s. 38; 1992, c. 11, s. 3; 1993, c. 45, s. 15; 1995, c. 19, s. 13; 1995, c. 22, ss. 16, 17, 25.

Mandatory prohibition order — Duration of prohibition order — Discretionary prohibition order — Duration of prohibition order — Definition of "release from imprisonment" — Reasons for the prohibition order — Reasons — Application of Criminal Code — Report

20.1 (1) Notwithstanding subsection 20(1), where a young person is found guilty of an offence referred to in any of paragraphs 109(1)(*a*) to (*d*) of the *Criminal Code*, the youth court shall, in addition to making any disposition referred to in subjection 20(1), make an order prohibiting the young person from possessing any firearm, cross-bow, prohibited weapon, restricted weapon, prohibited device, ammunition, prohibited ammunition and explosive substance during the period specified in the order as determined in accordance with subsection (2).

(2) An order made under subsection (1) begins on the day on which the order is made and ends not earlier than two years after the young person's release from custody after being found guilty of the offence or, if the young person is not then in custody or subject to custody, after the time the young person is found guilty of or discharged from the offence.

(3) Notwithstanding subsection 20(1), where a young person is found guilty of an offence referred to in paragraph 110(1)(*a*) or (*b*) of the *Criminal Code*, the youth court shall, in addition to making any disposition referred to in subsection 20(1), consider whether it is desirable, in the interests of the safety of the person or of any other person, to make an order prohibiting the person from possessing any firearm, cross-bow, prohibited weapon, restricted weapon, prohibited device, ammunition, prohibited ammunition or explosive substance, or all such things, and where the court decides that it is so desirable, the court shall so order.

(4) An order made under subsection (3) against a young person begins on the day on which the order is made and ends not later than two years after the young person's release from custody or, if the young person is not then in custody or subject to custody, after the time the young person is found guilty of or discharged from the offence.

(5) In paragraph (2)(*a*) and subsection (4), "release from custody" means a release from custody in accordance with this Act, other than a release from custody under subsection 35(1), and includes the commencement of conditional supervision or probation.

(6) Where a youth court makes an order under this section, it shall state its reasons for making the order in the record of the case and shall

(*a*) provide or cause to be provided a copy of the order, and

(*b*) on request, provide or cause to be provided a transcript or copy of the reasons for making the order

to the young person against whom the order was made, the young person's counsel and parents and the provincial director.

(7) Where the youth court does not make an order under subsection (3), or where the youth court does make such an order but does not prohibit the possession of everything referred to in that subsection, the youth court shall include in the record a statement of the youth court's reasons.

(8) Sections 113 to 117 of the *Criminal Code* apply in respect of any order made under this section.

(9) Before making any order referred to in section 113 of the *Criminal Code* in respect of a young person, the youth court may require the provincial director to cause to be prepared, and to submit to the youth court, a report on the young person. 1995, c. 39, s. 179. Not in force at date of publication.

Where a fine or other payment is ordered — Fine option program — Rates, crediting and other matters — Representations respecting orders under paras. 20(1)(c) to (f) — Notice of orders under paras. 20 (1)(c) to (f) — Consent of person to be compensated — Order for compensation or community service — Duration of order for service — Community service order — Application for further time to complete disposition.

21. (1) The youth court shall, in imposing a fine on a young person under paragraph 20(1)(*b*) or in making an order against a young person under paragraph 20(1)(*c*) or (*e*), have regard to the present and future means of the young person to pay.

(2) A young person against whom a fine is imposed under paragraph 20(1)(*b*) may discharge the fine in whole or in part by earning credits for work performed in a program established for that purpose

(*a*) by the Lieutenant Governor in Council of the province in which the fine was imposed; or

(*b*) by the Lieutenant Governor in Council of the province in which the young person resides, where an appropriate agreement is in effect between the government of that province and the government of the province in which the fine was imposed.

(3) A program referred to in subsection (2) shall determine the rate at which credits are earned and may provide for the manner of crediting any amounts earned against the fine and any other matters necessary for or incidental to carrying out the program.

(4) In considering whether to make an order under paragraphs 20(1)(*c*) to (*f*), the youth court may consider any representations made by the person who would be compensated or to whom restitution or payment would be made.

(5) Where the youth court makes an order under paragraphs 20(1)(*c*) to (*f*), it shall cause notice of the terms of the order to be given to the person who is to be compensated or to whom restitution or payment is to be made.

(6) No order can be made under paragraph 20(1)(*f*) unless the youth court has secured the consent of the person to be compensated.

(7) No order may be made under paragraph 20(1)(*f*) or (*g*) unless the youth court

(*a*) is satisfied that the young person against whom the order is made is a suitable candidate for such an order; and

(*b*) is satisfied that the order does not interfere with the normal hours of work or education of the young person.

(8) No order may be made under paragraph 20(1)(*f*) or (*g*) to perform personal or community services unless those services can be completed in two hundred and forty hours or less and within twelve months of the date of the order.

(9) No order may be made under paragraph 20(1)(*g*) unless

(*a*) the community service to be performed is part of a program that is approved by the provincial director, or

(*b*) the youth court is satisfied that the person or organization for whom the community service is to be performed has agreed to its performance.

(10) A youth court may, on application by or on behalf of the young person in respect of whom a disposition has been made under paragraphs 20(1)(*b*) to (*g*), allow further time for the completion of the disposition subject to any regulations made pursuant to paragraph 67(*b*) and to any rules made by the youth court pursuant to subsection 68(1). R.S. 1985, c. 24 (2nd Supp.), s. 15.

22. [Repealed 1995, c. 19, s. 14].

Conditions that must appear in probation orders — Conditions that may appear in probation orders — Communication of probation order to young person and parent — Copy of probation order to parent — Endorsement of order by young person — Validity of probation order — Commencement of probation order — Notice to appear — Warrant to arrest young person.

23. (1) The following conditions shall be included in a probation order made under paragraph 20(1)(*j*):

(*a*) that the young person bound by the probation order shall keep the peace and be of good behaviour; and

(*b*) that the young person appear before the youth court when required by the court to do so.

(*c*) [Repealed R.S. 1985, c. 24 (2d Supp.), s. 16(1).]

(2) A probation order made under paragraph 20(1)(*j*) may include such of the following conditions as the youth court considers appropriate in the circumstances of the case:

(*a*) that the young person bound by the probation order report to and be under the supervision of the provincial director or a person designated by the youth court;

(*a*.1) that the young person notify the clerk of the youth court, the provincial director or the youth worker assigned to his case of any change of address or any change in his place of employment, education or training;

(*b*) that the young person remain within the territorial jurisdiction of one or more courts named in the order;

(*c*) that the young person make reasonable efforts to obtain and maintain suitable employment;

(*d*) that the young person attend school or such other place of learning, training or recreation as is appropriate, if the court is satisfied that a suitable program is available for the young person at that place;

(*e*) that the young person reside with a parent, or such other adult as the court considers appropriate, who is willing to provide for the care and maintenance of the young person;

(*f*) that the young person reside in such place as the provincial director may specify; and

(*g*) that the young person comply with such other reasonable conditions set out in the order as the court considers desirable, including conditions for securing the good conduct of the young person and for preventing the commission by the young person of other offences.

(3) Where the youth court makes a probation order under paragraph 20(1)(*j*), it shall

(*a*) cause the order to be read by or to the young person bound by the probation order;

(*b*) explain or cause to be explained to the young person the purpose and effect of the order and ascertain that the young person understands it; and

(*c*) cause a copy of the order to be given to the young person and to a parent of the young person, if the parent is in attendance at the proceedings against the young person.

(4) Where the youth court makes a probation under paragraph 20(1)(*j*), it may cause a copy of the report to be given to a parent of the young person not in attendance at the proceedings against the young person if the parent is, in the opinion of the court, taking an active interest in the proceedings.

(5) After a probation order has been read by or to a young person and explained to him pursuant to subsection (3), the young person shall endorse the order acknowledging that he has received a copy of the order and acknowledging the fact that it has been explained to him.

(6) The failure of a young person to endorse a probation order pursuant to subsection (5) does not affect the validity of the order.

(7) A probation order made under paragraph 20(1)(*j*) comes into force

(*a*) on the date on which the order is made; or

(*b*) where the young person in respect of whom the order is made is committed to continuous custody, on the expiration of the period of custody.

(8) A young person may be given notice to appear before the youth court pursuant to paragraph (1)(*b*) orally or in writing.

(9) If a young person to whom a notice is given in writing to appear before the youth court pursuant to paragraph (1)(*b*) does not appear at the time and place named in the notice and it is proved that a copy of the notice was served on him, a youth court may issue a warrant to compel the appearance of the young person. R.S., c. 24 (2d Supp.), s. 16; c. 1 (4th Supp.), s. 39.

Conditions of custody — Factors — Pre-disposition report — Report dispensed with — Reasons.

24. (1) The youth court shall not commit a young person to custody under paragraph 20(1)(*k*) unless the court considers a committal to custody to be necessary for the protection of society having regard to the seriousness of the offence and the circumstances in which it was committed and having regard to the needs and circumstances of the young person.

(1.1) In making a determination under subsection (1), the youth court shall take the following into account:

(*a*) that an order of custody shall not be used as a substitute for appropriate child protection, health and other social measures;

(*b*) that a young person who commits an offence that does not involve serious personal injury should be held accountable to the victim and to society through non-custodial dispositions whenever appropriate; and

(c) that custody shall only be imposed when all available alternatives to custody that are reasonable in the circumstances have been considered.

(2) Subject to subsection (3), before making an order of committal to custody, the youth court shall consider a pre-disposition report.

(3) The youth court may, with the consent of the prosecutor and the young person or his counsel, dispense with the pre-disposition report required under subsection (2) if the youth court is satisfied, having regard to circumstances, that the report is unnecessary or that it would not be in the best interests of the young person to require one.

(4) Where the youth court makes a disposition in respect of a young person under paragraph 20(1)(k), the youth court shall state the reasons why any other disposition or dispositions under subsection 20(1), without the disposition under paragraph 20(1)(k), would not have been adequate. 1995, c. 19, s. 15.

Definitions — Youth court to specify type of custody — Provincial director to specify level of custody — Factors.
24.1 (1) In this section and sections 24.2, 24.3, 28 and 29,
''open custody'' means custody in
    (a) a community residential centre, group home, child care institution or forest or wilderness camp, or
    (b) any other like place or facility
designated by the Lieutenant Governor in Council of a province or his delegate as a place of open custody for the purposes of this Act, and includes a place or facility within a class of such places or facilities so designated;
''secure custody'' means custody in a place or facility designated by the Lieutenant Governor in Council of a province for the secure containment or restraint of young persons, and includes a place or facility within a class of such places or facilities so designated.

(2) Subject to subsection (3), where the youth court commits a young person to custody under paragraph 20(1)(k) or (k.1) or makes an order under subsection 26.1(1) or paragraph 26.6(2)(b), it shall specify in the order whether the custody is to be open custody or secure custody.

(3) In a province in which the Lieutenant Governor in Council has designated the provincial director to determine the level of custody, the provincial director shall, where a young person is committed to custody under paragraph 20(1)(k) or (k.1) or an order is made under subsection 26.1(1) or paragraph 26.6(2)(b), specify whether the young person shall be placed in open custody or secure custody.

(4) In deciding whether a young person shall be placed in open custody or secure custody, the youth court or the provincial director shall take into account the following factors:
    (a) that a young person should be placed in a level of custody involving the least degree of containment and restraint, having regard to
        (i) the seriousness of the offence in respect of which the young person was committed to custody and the circumstances in which that offence was committed,
        (ii) the needs and circumstances of the young person, including proximity to family, school, employment and support services,
        (iii) the safety of other young persons in custody, and
        (iv) the interests of society;
    (b) that the level of custody should allow for the best possible match of programs to the young person's needs and behaviour, having regard to the findings of any assessment in respect of the young person;
    (c) the likelihood of escape if the young person is placed in open custody; and
    (d) the recommendations, if any, of the youth court or the provincial director, as the case may be. R.S. 1985, c. 24 (2d Supp.), s. 17; 1992, c. 11, s. 4; 1995, c. 19, s. 16.

Place of custody — Warrant of committal — Exception — Young person to be held separate from adults — Subsection 7(2) applies — Transfer — Transfer to open custody — youth court — No transfer to secure custody — youth court — Exception — transfer to secure custody — youth court — Transfer to open custody — provincial director — Transfer to secure custody — provincial director — Notice — Where application for review is made — Interim custody.

24.2 (1) Subject to this section and sections 24.3 and 24.5, a young person who is committed to custody shall be placed in open custody or secure custody, as specified pursuant to subsection 24.1(2) or (3), at such place or facility as the provincial director may specify.

(2) Where a young person is committed to custody, the youth court shall issue or cause to be issued a warrant of committal.

(3) A young person who is committed to custody may, in the course of being transferred from custody to the court or from the court to custody, be held under the supervision and control of a peace officer or in such place of temporary detention referred to in subsection 7(1) as the provincial director may specify.

(4) Subject to this section and section 24.5, a young person who is committed to custody shall be held separate and apart from any adult who is detained or held in custody.

(5) Subsection 7(2) applies, with such modifications as the circumstances require, in respect of a person held in a place of temporary detention pursuant to subsection (3).

(6) A young person who is committed to custody may, during the period of custody, be transferred by the provincial director from one place or facility of open custody to another or from one place or facility of secure custody to another.

(7) No young person who is committed to secure custody pursuant to subsection 24.1(2) may be transferred to a place or facility of open custody except in accordance with sections 28 to 31.

(8) Subject to subsection (9), no young person who is committed to open custody pursuant to subsection 24.1(2) may be transferred to a place or facility of secure custody.

(9) Where a young person is placed in open custody pursuant to subsection 24.1(2), the provincial director may transfer the young person from a place or facility of open custody to a place or facility of secure custody for a period not exceeding fifteen days if

(*a*) the young person escapes or attempts to escape lawful custody; or

(*b*) the transfer is, in the opinion of the provincial director, necessary for the safety of the young person or the safety of others in the place or facility of open custody.

(10) The provincial director may transfer a young person from a place or facility of secure custody to a place or facility of open custody when the provincial director is satisfied that the needs of the young person and the interests of society would be better served thereby.

(11) The provincial director may transfer a young person from a place or facility of open custody to a place or facility of secure custody when the provincial director is satisfied that the needs of the young person and the interests of society would be better served thereby

(*a*) having considered the factors set out in subsection 24.1(4); and

(*b*) having determined that there has been a material change in circumstances since the young person was placed in open custody.

(12) The provincial director shall cause a notice in writing of the decision to transfer a young person under subsection (11) to be given to the young person and the young person's parents and set out in that notice the reasons for the transfer.

(13) Where an application for review under section 28.1 of a transfer under subsection (11) is made to a youth court,

(*a*) the provincial director shall cause such notice as may be directed by rules of court applicable to the youth court or, in the absence of such direction, at least five clear days notice of the review to be given in writing to the young person and the young person's parents; and

(*b*) the youth court shall forthwith, after the notice required under paragraph (*a*) is given, review the transfer.

(14) Where an application for review under section 28.1 of a transfer under subsection (11) is made to a youth court, the young person shall remain in a place or facility of secure custody until the review is heard by the youth court unless the provincial director directs otherwise. R.S. 1985, c. 24 (2d Supp.), s. 17; 1995, c. 19, s. 17.

Consecutive dispositions of custody — Concurrent dispositions of custody.

24.3 (1) Where a young person is committed to open custody and secure custody pursuant to subsection 24.1(2), any portions of which dispositions are to be served consecutively, the disposition of secure custody shall be served first without regard to the order in which the dispositions were imposed.

(2) Where a young person is committed to open custody and secure custody pursuant to subsection 24.1(2), any portions of which dispositions are to be served concurrently, the

concurrent portions of the dispositions shall be served in secure custody. R.S. 1985, c. 24 (2d Supp.), s. 17; 1995, c. 19, s. 18.

Committal to custody deemed continuous — Availability of place of intermittent custody.
24.4 (1) A young person who is committed to custody under paragraph 20(1)(*k*) shall de deemed to be committed to continuous custody unless the youth court specifies otherwise.

(2) Before making an order of committal to intermittent custody under paragraph 20(1)(*k*), the youth court shall require the prosecutor to make available to the court for its consideration a report of the provincial director as to the availability of a place of custody in which an order of intermittent custody can be enforced and, where the report discloses that no such place of custody is available, the court shall not make the order. R.S. 1985, c. 24 (2d Supp.), s. 17.

Transfer to adult facility — Where disposition and sentence concurrent.
24.5 (1) Where a young person is committed to custody under paragraph 20(1)(*k*) or (*k*.1) the youth court may, on application of the provincial director made at any time after the young person attains the age of eighteen years, after affording the young person an opportunity to be heard, authorize the provincial director to direct that the young person serve the disposition or the remaining portion thereof in a provincial correctional facility for adults, if the court considers it to be in the best interests of the young person or in the public interest, but in that event, the provisions of this Act shall continue to apply in respect of that person.

(2) Where a young person is committed to custody under paragraph 20(1)(*k*) or (*k*.1) and is concurrently under sentence of imprisonment imposed in ordinary court, the young person may, in the discretion of the provincial director, serve the disposition and sentence, or any portions thereof, in a place of custody for young persons, in a provincial correctional facility for adults or, where the unexpired portion of the sentence is two years or more, in a penitentiary. R.S. 1985, c. 24 (2nd Supp.), s. 17; 1992, c. 11, s. 5.

Transfer of disposition — No transfer outside province before appeal completed — Transfer to a province where person is adult.
25. (1) Where a disposition has been made under paragraphs 20(1)(*b*) to (*g*) or paragraph 20(1)(*j*) or (*l*) in respect of a young person and the young person or a parent with whom the young person resides is or becomes a resident of a territorial division outside the jurisdiction of the youth court that made the disposition, whether in the same or in another province, a youth court judge in the territorial division in which the disposition was made may, on the application of the Attorney General or an agent of the Attorney General or on the application of the young person or the young person's parent with the consent of the Attorney General or an agent of the Attorney General, transfer the disposition and such portion of the record of the case as is appropriate to a youth court in the other territorial division, and all subsequent proceedings relating to the case shall thereafter be carried out and enforced by that court.

(2) No disposition may be transferred from one province to another under this section until the time for an appeal against the disposition or the finding on which the disposition was based has expired or until all proceedings in respect of any such appeal have been completed.

(3) Where an application is made under subsection (1) to transfer the disposition of a young person to a province in which the young person is an adult, a youth court judge may, with the consent of the Attorney General, transfer the disposition and the record of the case to the youth court in the province to which the transfer is sought, and the youth court to which the case is transferred shall have full jurisdiction in respect of the disposition as if that court had made the disposition, and the person shall be further dealt with in accordance with this Act. R.S. 1985, c. 24 (2d Supp.), s. 18; 1995, c. 19, s. 19.

Interprovincial arrangements for probation or custody — Youth court retains jurisdiction — Waiver of jurisdiction.
25.1 (1) Where a disposition has been made under paragraphs 20(1)(*j*) to (*k*.1) in respect of a young person, the disposition in one province may be dealt with in any other province pursuant to any agreement that may have been made between those provinces.

(2) Subject to subsection (3), where a disposition made in respect of a young person is dealt with pursuant to this section in a province other than that in which the disposition was

made, the youth court of the province in which the disposition was made shall, for all purposes of this Act, retain exclusive jurisdiction over the young person as if the disposition were dealt with within that province, and any warrant or process issued in respect of the young person may be executed or served in any place in Canada outside the province where the disposition was made as if it were executed or served in that province.

(3) Where a disposition made in respect of a young person is dealt with pursuant to this section in a province other than that in which the disposition was made, the youth court of the province in which the disposition was made may, with the consent in writing of the Attorney General of that province or his delegate and the young person, waive its jurisdiction, for the purpose of any proceeding under this Act, to the youth court of the province in which the disposition is dealt with, in which case the youth court in the province in which the disposition is so dealt with shall have full jurisdiction in respect of the disposition as if that court had made the disposition. R.S. 1985, c. 24 (2d Supp.), s. 19; 1992, c. 11, s. 6; 1995, c. 19, s. 20.

Failure to comply with disposition.
 26. A person who is subject to a disposition made under paragraphs 20(1)(*b*) to (*g*) or paragraph 20(1)(*j*) or (*l*) and who wilfully fails or refuses to comply with that order is guilty of an offence punishable on summary conviction. R.S. 1985, c. 24 (2nd Supp.), s. 19.

Continuation of custody — Idem — Factors — Youth court to order appearance of young person — Report — Written or oral report — Provisions apply — Notice of hearing — Statement of right to counsel — Service of notice — Where notice not given — Reasons — Review provisions apply — Where application denied.
 26.1 (1) Where a young person is held in custody pursuant to a disposition made under paragraph 20(1)(*k*.1)and an application is made to the youth court by the Attorney General, or the Attorney General's agent, within a reasonable time prior to the expiration of the period of custody, the provincial director of the province in which the young person is held in custody shall cause the young person to be brought before the youth court and the youth court may, after affording both parties and the parents of the young person an opportunity to be heard and if it is satisfied that there are reasonable grounds to believe that the young person is likely to commit an offence causing the death of or serious harm to another person prior to the expiration of the disposition the young person is then serving, order that the young person remain in custody for a period not exceeding the remainder of the disposition.

(1.1) Where the hearing for an application under subsection (1) cannot be completed before the expiration of the period of custody, the court may order that the young person remain in custody pending the determination of the application if the court is satisfied that the application was made in a reasonable time, having regard to all the circumstances, and that there are compelling reasons for keeping the young person in custody.

(2) For the purpose of determining an application under subsection (1), the youth court shall take into consideration any factor that is relevant to the case of the young person including, without limiting the generality of the foregoing,

    (*a*) evidence of a pattern of persistent violent behaviour and, in particular,
        (i) the number of offences committed by the young person that caused physical or psychological harm to any other person,
        (ii) the young person's difficulties in controlling violent impulses to the point of endangering the safety of any other person,
        (iii) the use of weapons in the commission of any offence,
        (iv) explicit threats of violence,
        (v) behaviour of a brutal nature associated with the commission of any offence, and
        (vi) a substantial degree of indifference on the part of the young person as to the reasonably forseeable consequences, to other persons, of the young person's behaviour,
    (*b*) psychiatric or psychological evidence that a physical or mental illness or disorder of the young person is of such a nature that the young person is likely to commit, prior to the expiration of the disposition the young person is then serving, an offence causing the death of or serious harm to another person;

(c) reliable information that satisfies the youth court that the young person is planning to commit, prior to the expiration of the disposition the young person is then serving, an offence causing the death of or serious harm to another person; and

(d) the availability of supervision programs in the community that would offer adequate protection to the public from the risk that the young person might otherwise present until the expiration of the disposition the young person is then serving.

(3) Where a provincial director fails to cause a young person to be brought before the youth court under subsection (1), the youth court shall order the provincial director to cause the young person to be brought before the youth court forthwith.

(4) For the purpose of determining an application under subsection (1), the youth court shall require the provincial director to cause to be prepared, and to submit to the youth court, a report setting out any information of which the provincial director is aware with respect to the factors referred to in subsection (2) that may be of assistance to the court.

(5) A report referred to in subsection (4) shall be in writing unless it cannot reasonably be committed to writing, in which case it may, with leave of the youth court, be submitted orally in court.

(6) Subsections 14(4) to (10) apply, with such modifications as the circumstances require, in respect of a report referred to in subsection (4).

(7) Where an application is made under subsection (1) in respect of a young person, the Attorney General or the Attorney General's agent shall cause such notice as may be directed by rules of court applicable to the youth court or, in the absence of such direction, at least five clear days notice of the hearing to be given in writing to the young person and the young person's parents and the provincial director.

(8) Any notice given to a parent under subsection (7) shall include a statement that the young person has the right to be represented by counsel.

(9) A notice under subsection (7) may be served personally or may be sent by registered mail.

(10) Where notice under subsection (7) is not given in accordance with this section, the youth court may

(a) adjourn the hearing and order that the notice be given in such manner and to such person as it directs; or

(b) dispense with the giving of the notice where, in the opinion of the youth court, having regard to the circumstances, the giving of the notice may be dispensed with.

(11) Where a youth court makes an order under subsection (1), it shall state its reasons for the order in the record of the case and shall

(a) provide or cause to be provided a copy of the order, and

(b) on request, provide or cause to be provided a transcript or copy of the reasons for the order

to the young person in respect of whom the order was made, the counsel and parents of the young person, the Attorney General or the Attorney General's agent, the provincial director and the review board, if any has been established or designated.

(12) Subsections 16(9) to (11) apply, with such modifications as the circumstances require, in respect of an order made, or the refusal to make an order, under subsection (1).

(13) Where an application under subsection (1) is denied, the court may, with the consent of the young person, the Attorney General and the provincial director, proceed as though the young person had been brought before the court as required under subsection 26.2(1). 1992, c. 11, s. 7.

Conditional supervision — Conditions to be included in order — Other conditions — Temporary conditions — Conditions to be set at first opportunity — Report — Provisions apply — Idem.

26.2 (1) The provincial director of the province in which a young person is held in custody pursuant to a disposition made under paragraph 20(1)(k.1) or, where applicable, an order made under subsection 26.1(1), shall cause the young person to be brought before the youth court at least one month prior to the expiration of the period of custody and the court shall, after affording the young person an opportunity to be heard, by order, set the conditions of the young person's conditional supervision.

(2) In setting conditions for the purposes of subsection (1), the youth court shall include in the order the following conditions, namely, that the young person

(*a*) keep the peace and be of good behaviour;

(*b*) appear before the youth court when required by the court to do so;

(*c*) report to the provincial director immediately on release, and thereafter be under the supervision of the provincial director or a person designated by the youth court;

(*d*) inform the provincial director immediately on being arrested or questioned by the police;

(*e*) report to the police, or any named individual, as instructed by the provincial director;

(*f*) advise the provincial director of the young person's address of residence on release and after release report immediately to the clerk of the youth court or the provincial director any change

    (i) in that address,

    (ii) in the young person's normal occupation, including employment, vocational or educational training and volunteer work,

    (iii) in the young person's family or financial situation, and

    (iv) that may reasonably be expected to affect the young person's ability to comply with the conditions of the order;

(*g*) not own, possess or have the control of any weapon, as defined in section 2 of the *Criminal Code*, except as authorized by the order; and

(*g*) not own, possess or have the control of any weapon, ammunition, prohibited ammunition, prohibited device or explosive substance, except as authorized by the order; and

1995, c. 39, s. 180. Not in force at date of publication.

(*h*) comply with such reasonable instructions as the provincial director considers necessary in respect of any condition of the conditional supervision in order to prevent a breach of that condition or to protect society.

(3) In setting conditions for the purposes of subsection (1), the youth court may include in the order the following conditions, namely, that the young person

(*a*) on release, travel directly to the young person's place of residence, or to such other place as is noted in the order;

(*b*) make reasonable efforts to obtain and maintain suitable employment;

(*c*) attend school or such other place of learning, training or recreation as is appropriate, if the court is satisfied that a suitable program is available for the young person at such a place;

(*d*) reside with a parent, or such other adult as the court considers appropriate, who is willing to provide for the care and maintenance of the young person;

(*e*) reside in such place as the provincial director may specify;

(*f*) remain within the territorial jurisdiction of one or more courts named in the order; and

(*g*) comply with such other reasonable conditions set out in the order as the court considers desirable, including conditions for securing the good conduct of the young person and for preventing the commission by the young person of other offences.

(4) Where a provincial director is required under subsection (1) to cause a young person to be brought before the youth court but cannot do so for reasons beyond the young person's control, the provincial director shall so advise the youth court and the court shall, by order, set such temporary conditions for the young person's conditional supervision as are appropriate in the circumstances.

(5) Where an order is made under subsection (4), the provincial director shall bring the young person before the youth court as soon thereafter as the circumstances permit and the court shall then set the conditions of the young person's conditional supervision.

(6) For the purpose of setting conditions under this section, the youth court shall require the provincial director to cause to be prepared, and to submit to the youth court, a report setting out any information that may be of assistance to the court.

(7) Subsections 26.1(3) and (5) to (10) apply, with such modifications as the circumstances require, in respect of any proceedings held pursuant to subsection (1).

(8) Subsections 16(9) to (11) and 23(3) to (9) apply, with such modifications as the circumstances require, in respect of an order made under subsection (1). 1992, c. 11, s. 7.

Suspension of conditional supervision.

26.3 (1) Where the provincial director has reasonable grounds to believe that a young person has breached or is about to breach a condition of an order made under subsection 26.2(1), the provincial director may, in writing,

    (*a*) suspend the conditional supervision; and

    (*b*) order that the young person be remanded to such place of custody as the provincial director considers appropriate until a review is conducted under section 26.5 and, if applicable, section 26.6. 1992, c. 11, s. 7.

Apprehension — Warrants — Peace officer may arrest — Requirement to bring before provincial director — Release or remand in custody.

26.4 (1) Where the conditional supervision of a young person is suspended under section 26.3, the provincial director may issue a warrant in writing, authorizing the apprehension of the young person and, until the young person is apprehended, the young person is deemed not to be continuing to serve the disposition the young person is then serving.

(2) A warrant issued under subsection (1) shall be executed by any peace officer to whom it is given at any place in Canada and has the same force and effect in all parts of Canada as if it had been originally issued or subsequently endorsed by a provincial court judge or other lawful authority having jurisdiction in the place where it is executed.

(3) Where a peace officer believes on reasonable grounds that a warrant issued under subsection (1) is in force in respect of a young person, the peace officer may arrest the young person without the warrant at any place in Canada.

(4) Where a young person is arrested pursuant to subsection (3) and detained, the peace officer making the arrest shall cause the young person to be brought before the provincial director or a person designated by the provincial director

    (*a*) where the provincial director or the designated person is available within a period of twenty-four hours after the young person is arrested, without unreasonable delay and in any event within that period; and

    (*b*) where the provincial director or the designated person is not available within the period referred to in paragraph (*a*), as soon as possible.

(5) Where a young person is brought, pursuant to subsection (4), before the provincial director or a person designated by the provincial director, the provincial director or the designated person,

    (*a*) if not satisfied that there are reasonable grounds to believe that the young person is the young person in respect of whom the warrant referred to in subsection (1) was issued, shall release the young person; or

    (*b*) if satisfied that there are reasonable grounds to believe that the young person is the young person in respect of whom the warrant referred to in subsection (1) was issued, may remand the young person in custody to await execution of the warrant, but if no warrant for the young person's arrest is executed within a period of six days after the time the young person is remanded in such custody, the person in whose custody the young person then is shall release the young person. 1992, c. 11, s. 7.

Review by provincial director.

26.5 Forthwith after the remand to custody of a young person whose conditional supervision has been suspended under section 26.3, or forthwith after being informed of the arrest of such a young person, the provincial director shall review the case and, within forty-eight hours, cancel the suspension of the conditional supervision or refer the case to the youth court for a review under section 26.6. 1992, c. 11, s. 7.

Review by Youth Court — Order — Reasons — Provisions apply — Idem.

26.6 (1) Where the case of a young person is referred to the youth court under section 26.5, the provincial director shall, as soon as is practicable, cause the young person to be brought before the youth court, and the youth court shall, after affording the young person an opportunity to be heard,

    (*a*) if the court is not satisfied on reasonable grounds that the young person has breached or was about to breach a condition of the conditional supervision, cancel the suspension of the conditional supervision; or

    (*b*) if the court is satisfied on reasonable grounds that the young person has breached or was about to breach a condition of the conditional supervision, review the decision of the provincial director to suspend the conditional supervision and make an order under subsection (2).

(2) On completion of a review under subsection (1), the youth court shall order

(*a*) the cancellation of the suspension of the conditional supervision, and where the court does so, the court may vary the conditions of the conditional supervision or impose new conditions; or

(*b*) the continuation of the suspension of the conditional supervision for such period of time, not to exceed the remainder of the disposition the young person is then serving, as the court considers appropriate, and where the court does so, the court shall order that the young person remain in custody.

(3) Where a youth court makes an order under subsection (2), it shall state its reasons for the order in the record of the case and shall

(*a*) provide or cause to be provided a copy of the order, and

(*b*) on request, provide or cause to be provided a transcript or copy of the reasons for the order

to the young person in respect of whom the order was made, the counsel and parents of the young person, the Attorney General or the Attorney General's agent, the provincial director and the review board, if any has been established or designated.

(4) Subsections 26.1(3) and (5) to (10) and 26.2(6) apply, with such modifications as the circumstances require, in respect of a review under this section.

(5) Subsections 16(9) to (11) apply, with such modifications as the circumstances require, in respect of an order made under subsection (2). 1992, c. 11, s. 7.

APPEALS

Appeals for indictable offences — Appeals for summary conviction offences — Appeals where offences are tried jointly — Deemed election — Where the youth court is a superior court — Where the youth court is a county or district court — Appeal to the Supreme Court of Canada — No appeal from disposition on review.

27. (1) An appeal lies under this Act in respect of an indictable offence or an offence that the Attorney General or his agent elects to proceed with as an indictable offence in accordance with Part XXI of the *Criminal Code*, which Part applies with such modifications as the circumstances require.

(1.1) An appeal lies under this Act in respect of an offence punishable on summary conviction or an offence that the Attorney General or his agent elects to proceed with as an offence punishable on summary conviction in accordance with Part XXVII of the *Criminal Code*, which Part applies with such modifications as the circumstances require.

(1.2) An appeal involving one or more indictable offences and one or more summary conviction offences that are tried jointly or in respect of which dispositions are jointly made lies under this Act in accordance with Part XXI of the *Criminal Code*, which applies with such modifications as the circumstances require.

(2) For the purpose of appeals under this Act, where no election is made in respect of an offence that may be prosecuted by indictment or proceeded with by way of summary conviction, the Attorney General or his agent shall be deemed to have elected to proceed with the offence as an offence punishable on summary conviction.

(3) In any province where the youth court is a superior court, an appeal under subsection (1.1) shall be made to the court of appeal of the province.

(4) In any province where the youth court is a county or district court, an appeal under subsection (1.1) shall be made to the superior court of the province.

(5) No appeal lies pursuant to subsection (1) from a judgment of the court of appeal in respect of a finding of guilt or an order dismissing an information to the Supreme Court of Canada unless leave to appeal is granted by the Supreme Court of Canada within twenty-one days after the judgment of the court of appeal is pronounced or within such extended time as the Supreme Court of Canada or a judge thereof may, for special reasons, allow.

(6) No appeal lies from a disposition under sections 28 to 32. R.S. 1985, c. 24 (2d Supp.), s. 20; 1995, c. 19, s. 21.

REVIEW OF DISPOSITIONS

Automatic review of disposition involving custody — Idem — Optional review of disposition involving custody — Grounds for review under subsection (3) — No review where appeal pending — Youth court may order appearance of young person for review — Progress report — Additional information in progress report — Written or oral report — Provisions of subsections 14(4) to (10) to apply — Notice of review from provincial director — Notice of review from person requesting it — Statement of right to counsel — Service of notice — Notice may be waived — Where notice not given — Decision of the youth court after review.

28. (1) Where a young person is committed to custody pursuant to a disposition made in respect of an offence for a period exceeding one year, the provincial director of the province in which the young person is held in custody shall cause the young person to be brought before the youth court forthwith at the end of one year from the date of the most recent disposition made in respect of the offence, and the youth court shall review the disposition.

(2) Where a young person is committed to custody pursuant to dispositions made in respect of more than one offence for a total period exceeding one year, the provincial director of the province in which the young person is held in custody shall cause the young person to be brought before the youth court forthwith at the end of one year from the date of the earliest disposition made, and the youth court shall review the dispositions.

(3) Where a young person is committed to custody pursuant to a disposition made under subsection 20(1) in respect of an offence, the provincial director may, on the provincial director's own initiative, and shall, on the request of the young person, the young person's parent or the Attorney General or an agent of the Attorney General, on any of the grounds set out in subsection (4), cause the young person to be brought before a youth court

    (*a*) where the committal to custody is for a period not exceeding one year, once at any time after the expiration of the greater of

        (i) thirty days after the date of the disposition made under subsection 20(1) in respect of the offence, and

        (ii) one third of the period of the disposition made under subsection 20(1) in respect of the offence, and

    (*b*) where the committal to custody is for a period exceeding one year, at any time after

six months after the date of the most recent disposition made in respect of the offence, or, with leave of a youth court judge, at any other time, and where a youth court is satisfied that there are grounds for the review under subsection (4), the court shall review the disposition.

(4) A disposition made in respect of a young person may be reviewed under subsection (3)

    (*a*) on the ground that the young person has made sufficient progress to justify a change in disposition;

    (*b*) on the ground that the circumstances that led to the committal to custody have changed materially;

    (*c*) on the ground that new services or programs are available that were not available at the time of the disposition;

    (*c*.1) on the ground that the opportunities for rehabilitation are now greater in the community; or

    (*d*) on such other grounds as the youth court considers appropriate.

(5) No review of a disposition in respect of which an appeal has been taken shall be made under this section until all proceedings in respect of any such appeal have been completed.

(6) Where a provincial director is required under subsections (1) to (3) to cause a young person to be brought before the youth court and fails to do so, the youth court may, on application made by the young person, his parent or the Attorney General or his agent, or on its own motion, order the provincial director to cause the young person to be brought before the youth court.

(7) The youth court shall, before reviewing under this section a disposition made in respect of a young person, require the provincial director to cause to be prepared, and to submit to the youth court, a progress report on the performance of the young person since the disposition took effect.

(8) A person preparing a progress report in respect of a young person may include in the report such information relating to the personal and family history and present environment of the young person as he considers advisable.

(9) A progress report shall be in writing unless it cannot reasonably be committed to writing, in which case it may, with leave of the youth court, be submitted orally in court.

(10) The provisions of subsections 14(4) to (10) apply, with such modifications as the circumstances require, in respect of progress reports.

(11) Where a disposition made in respect of a young person is to be reviewed under subsection (1) or (2), the provincial director shall cause such notice as may be directed by rules of court applicable to the youth court or, in the absence of such direction, at least five clear days notice of the review to be given in writing to the young person, his parents and the Attorney General or his agent.

(12) Where a review of a disposition made in respect of a young person is requested under subsection (3), the person requesting the review shall cause such notice as may be directed by rules of court applicable to the youth court or, in the absence of such direction, at least five clear days notice of the review to be given in writing to the young person, his parents and the Attorney General or his agent.

(13) Any notice given to a parent under subsection (11) or (12) shall include a statement that the young person whose disposition is to be reviewed has the right to be represented by counsel.

(14) A notice under subsection (11) or (12) may be served personally or may be sent by registered mail.

(15) Any of the persons entitled to notice under subsection (11) or (12) may waive the right to that notice.

(16) Where notice under subsection (11) or (12) is not given in accordance with this section, the youth court may

(*a*) adjourn the proceedings and order that the notice be given in such manner and to such person as it directs; or

(*b*) dispense with the notice where, in the opinion of the court, having regard to the circumstances, notice may be dispensed with.

(17) Where a youth court reviews under this section a disposition made in respect of a young person, it may, after affording the young person, his parent, the Attorney General or his agent and the provincial director an opportunity to be heard, having regard to the needs of the young person and the interests of society,

(*a*) confirm the disposition;

(*b*) where the young person is in secure custody pursuant to subsection 24.1(2), by order direct that the young person be placed in open custody; or

(*c*) release the young person from custody and place the young person

(i) on probation in accordance with section 23 for a period not exceeding the remainder of the period for which the young person was committed to custody, or

(ii) under conditional supervision in accordance with the procedure set out in section 26.2, with such modifications as the circumstances require, for a period not exceeding the remainder of the disposition the young person is then serving.

(18) [Repealed R.S. 1985, c. 24 (2d Supp.), s. 21.] R.S. 1985, c. 24 (2d Supp.), s. 21; 1992, c. 11, s. 8; 1995, c. 19, s. 22.

Application to court for review of level of custody — Report — Provisions apply — Decision of the youth court — Decision is final.

28.1 (1) Where a young person is placed in secure custody pursuant to subsection 24.1(3) or transferred to secure custody pursuant to subsection 24.2(11), the youth court shall review the level of custody if an application therefor is made by the young person or the young person's parent.

(2) The youth court shall, before conducting a review under this section, require the provincial director to cause to be prepared and to submit to the youth court, a report setting out the reasons for the placement or transfer.

(3) The provisions of subsections 14(4) to (10) apply, with such modifications as the circumstances require, in respect of the report referred to in subsection (2), and the provisions of subsections 28(11) to (16) apply, with such modifications as the circumstances require, to every review under this section.

(4) Where the youth court conducts a review under this section, it may, after affording the young person, the young person's parents and the provincial director an opportunity to

be heard, confirm or alter the level of custody, having regard to the needs of the young person and the interests of society.

(5) A decision of the youth court on a review under this section in respect of any particular placement or transfer is, subject to any subsequent order made pursuant to a review under section 28 or 29, final. 1995, c. 19, s. 23.

Recommendation of provincial director for transfer to open custody or for probation — Contents of notice — Application to court for review of recommendation — Subsections 28(5), (7) to (10) and (12) to (17) apply — Where no application for review made under subsection (2) — Conditions in probation order — Notice where no direction made — Provincial director may request review — Where the provincial director requests a review.

29. (1) Where a young person is held in custody pursuant to a disposition, the provincial director may, if he is satisfied that the needs of the young person and the interests of society would be better served thereby, cause notice in writing to be given to the young person, his parent and the Attorney General or his agent that he recommends that the young person

(*a*) be transferred from a place or facility of secure custody to a place or facility of open custody, where the young person is held in a place or facility of secure custody pursuant to subsection 24.1(2), or

(*b*) be released from custody and placed on probation or, where the young person is in custody pursuant to a disposition made under paragraph 20(1)(*k*.1), placed under conditional supervision.

and give a copy of the notice to the youth court.

(1.1) The provincial director shall include in any notice given under subsection (1) the reasons for the recommendation and

(*a*) in the case of a recommendation that the young person be placed on probation, the conditions that the provincial director would recommend be attached to a probation order; and

(*b*) in the case of a recommendation that the young person be placed under conditional supervision, the conditions that the provincial director would recommend be set pursuant to section 26.2.

(2) Where notice of a recommendation is made under subsection (1) with respect to a disposition made in respect of a young person, the youth court shall, if an application for review is made by the young person, his parent or the Attorney General or his agent within ten days after service of the notice, forthwith review the disposition.

(3) Subject to subsection (4), subsections 28(5), (7) to (10) and (12) to (17) apply, with such modifications as the circumstances require, in respect of reviews made under this section and any notice required under subsection 28(12) shall be given to the provincial director.

(4) A youth court that receives a notice under subsection (1) shall, if no application for a review is made under subsection (2),

(*a*) in the case of a recommendation that a young person be transferred from a place or facility of secure custody to a place or facility of open custody, order that the young person be so transferred;

(*b*) in the case of a recommendation that a young person be released from custody and placed on probation, release the young person and place him on probation in accordance with section 23;

(*b*.1) in the case of a recommendation that a young person be released from custody and placed under conditional supervision, release the young person and place the young person under conditional supervision in accordance with section 26.2, having regard to the recommendations of the provincial director; or

(*c*) where the court deems it advisable, make no direction under this subsection;

and for greater certainty, an order or direction under this subsection may be made without a hearing.

(4.1) Where the youth court places a young person on probation pursuant to paragraph (4)(*b*), the court shall include in the probation order such conditions referred to in section 23 as it considers advisable, having regard to the recommendations of the provincial director.

(4.2) Where a youth court, pursuant to paragraph (4)(*c*), makes no direction under subsection (4), it shall forthwith cause a notice of its decision to be given to the provincial director.

(4.3) Where the provincial director is given a notice under subsection (4.2), he may request a review under this section.

(5) Where the provincial director requests a review pursuant to subsection (4.3),

(a) the provincial director shall cause such notice as may be directed by rules of court applicable to the youth court or, in the absence of such direction, at least five clear days notice of the review to be given in writing to the young person, his parents and the Attorney General or his agent; and

(b) the youth court shall forthwith, after the notice required under paragraph (a) is given, review the disposition.

(6) [Repealed R.S. 1985, c. 24 (2d Supp.), s. 22.]

R.S. 1985, c. 24 (2d Supp.), s. 22; c. 1 (4th Supp.), s. 40; 1992, c. 11, s. 9; 1995, c. 19, s. 24.

Review board — Other duties of review board — Notice under section 29 — Notice of decision of review board — Decision of review board to take effect where no review — Decision respecting release from custody and probation — Decision respecting release from custody and conditional supervision.

30. (1) Where a review board is established or designated by a province for the purposes of this section, that board shall, subject to this section, carry out in that province the duties and functions of a youth court under sections 28 and 29, other than releasing a young person from custody and placing the young person on probation or under conditional supervision.

(2) Subject to this Act, a review board may carry out any duties or functions that are assigned to it by the province that established or designated it.

(3) Where a review board is established or designated by a province for the purposes of this section, the provincial director shall at the same time as any notice is given under subsection 29(1) cause a copy of the notice to be given to the review board.

(4) A review board shall cause notice of any decision made by it in respect of a young person pursuant to section 28 or 29 to be given forthwith in writing to the young person, his parents, the Attorney General or his agent and the provincial director, and a copy of the notice to be given to the youth court.

(5) Subject to subsection (6), any decision of a review board under this section shall take effect ten days after the decision is made unless an application for review is made under section 31.

(6) Where a review board decides that a young person should be released from custody and placed on probation, it shall so recommend to the youth court and, if no application for a review of the decision is made under section 31, the youth court shall forthwith on the expiration of the ten day period referred to in subsection (5) release the young person from custody and place him on probation in accordance with section 23, and shall include in the probation order such conditions referred to in that section as the court considers advisable having regard to the recommendations of the review board.

(7) Where a review board decides that a young person should be released from custody and placed under conditional supervision, it shall so recommend to the youth court and, if no application for a review of the decision is made under section 31, the youth court shall forthwith, on the expiration of the ten day period referred to in subsection (5), release the young person from custody and place the young person under conditional supervision in accordance with section 26.2, and shall include in the order under that section such conditions as the court considers advisable, having regard to the recommendations of the review board.

R.S. 1985, c. 24 (2nd Supp.), s. 23; 1992, c. 11, s. 10.

Review by youth court — Subsections 28(5), (7) to (10) and (12) to (17) apply.

31. (1) Where the review board reviews a disposition under section 30, the youth court shall, on the application of the young person in respect of whom the review was made, his parents, the Attorney General or his agent or the provincial director, made within ten days after the decision of the review board is made, forthwith review the decision.

(2) Subsections 28(5), (7) to (10) and (12) to (17) apply, with such modifications as the circumstances require, in respect of reviews made under this section and any notice required under subsection 28(12) shall be given to the provincial director.R.S. 1985, c. 1 (4th Supp.), s. 41.

Review of dispositions not involving custody — Review of other dispositions — Grounds for review — Progress report — Subsections 28(8) to (10) apply — Subsections 28(5) and (12) to (16) apply — Compelling appearance of young person — Decision of the youth court after review — New disposition not to be more onerous — Exception.

32. (1) Where a youth court has made a disposition in respect of a young person, other than or in addition to a disposition under paragraph 20(1)(*k*), and other than a disposition under paragraph 20(1)(*k.*1), the youth court shall, on the application of the young person, the young person's parents, the Attorney General or the Attorney General's agent or the provincial director, made at any time after six months from the date of the disposition or, with leave of a youth court judge, at any earlier time, review the disposition if the court is satisfied that there are grounds for a review under subsection (2).

(1) Where a youth court has made a disposition in respect of a young person, other than a disposition under paragraph 20(1)(*k*) or (*k.*1) or section 20.1, the youth court shall, on the application of the young person, the young person's parents, the Attorney General or the Attorney General's agent or the provincial director, made at any time after six months from the date of the disposition or, with leave of a youth court judge, at any earlier time, review the disposition if the court is satisfied that there are grounds for a review under subsection (2). 1995, c. 39, s. 181. Not in force at date of publication.

(2) A review of a disposition may be made under this section

(*a*) on the ground that the circumstances that led to the disposition have changed materially;

(*b*) on the ground that the young person in respect of whom the review is to be made is unable to comply with or is experiencing serious difficulty in complying with the terms of the disposition;

(*c*) on the ground that the terms of the disposition are adversely affecting the opportunities available to the young person to obtain services, education or employment; or

(*d*) on such other grounds as the youth court considers appropriate.

(3) The youth court may, before reviewing under this section a disposition made in respect of a young person, require the provincial director to cause to be prepared, and to submit to the youth court, a progress report on the performance of the young person since the disposition took effect.

(4) Subsections 28(8) to (10) apply, with such modifications as the circumstances require, in respect of any progress report required under subsection (3).

(5) Subsections 28(5) and (12) to (16) apply, with such modifications as the circumstances require, in respect of reviews made under this section and any notice required under subsection 28(12) shall be given to the provincial director.

(6) The youth court may, by summons or warrant, compel a young person in respect of whom a review is to be made under this section to appear before the youth court for the purposes of the review.

(7) Where a youth court reviews under this section a disposition made in respect of a young person, it may, after affording the young person, his parent, the Attorney General or his agent and the provincial director an opportunity to be heard,

(*a*) confirm the disposition;

(*b*) terminate the disposition and discharge the young person from any further obligation of the disposition; or

(*c*) vary the disposition or make such new disposition listed in section 20, other than a committal to custody, for such period of time, not exceeding the remainder of the period of the earlier disposition, as the court deems appropriate in the circumstances of the case.

(8) Subject to subsection (9), where a disposition made in respect of a young person is reviewed under this section, no disposition made under subsection (7) shall, without the consent of the young person, be more onerous than the remaining portion of the disposition reviewed.

(9) A youth court may under this section extend the time within which a disposition made under paragraphs 20(1)(*b*) to (*g*) is to be complied with by a young person where the court is satisfied that the young person requires more time to comply with the disposition, but in no case shall the extension be for a period of time that expires more than twelve months after the date the disposition would otherwise have expired.

(10), (11) [Repealed R.S. 1985, c. 24 (2d Supp.), s. 24.]

R.S. 1985, c. 24 (2d Supp.), s. 24; 1992, c. 11, s. 11.

33. [Repealed R.S. 1985, c. 24 (2d Supp.), s. 25.]

Review of order made under s. 20.1 — Grounds — Decision of review — New order not to be more onerous — Application of provisions.
   33. (1) A youth court or other court may, on application, review an order made under section 20.1 at any time after the circumstances set out in subsection 45(1) are realized in respect of any record in relation to the offence that resulted in the order being made.
   (2) In conducting a review under this section, the youth court or other court shall take into account
      (*a*) the nature and circumstances of the offence in respect of which the order was made; and
      (*b*) the safety of the young person and of other persons.
   (3) Where a youth court or other court conducts a review under this section, it may, after affording the young person, one of the young person's parents, the Attorney General or an agent of the Attorney General and the provincial director an opportunity to be heard,
      (*a*) confirm the order;
      (*b*) revoke the order; or
      (*c*) vary the order as it considers appropriate in the circumstances of the case.
   (4) No variation of an order made under paragraph 3(*c*) may be more onerous than the order being reviewed.
   (5) Subsections 32(3) to (5) apply, with such modifications as the circumstances require, in respect of a review under this section. 1995, c. 39, s. 182. Not in force at date of publication.

Sections 20 to 26 apply to dispositions on review — Orders are dispositions.
   34. (1) Subject to sections 28 to 32, subsections 20(2) to (8) and sections 21 to 25.1 apply, with such modifications as the circumstances require, in respect of dispositions made under sections 28 to 32.
   (2) Orders under subsections 26.1(1) and 26.2(1) and paragraph 26.6(2)(*b*) are deemed to be dispositions for the purposes of section 28. R.S. 1985, c. 24 (2d Supp.), s. 25; 1992, c. 11, s. 12.

TEMPORARY RELEASE FROM CUSTODY

Temporary absence or day release — Limitation — Revocation of authorization for release — Arrest and return to custody — Prohibition.
   35. (1) The provincial director of a province may, subject to any terms or conditions that he considers desirable, authorize a young person committed to custody in the province pursuant to a disposition made under this Act
      (*a*) to be temporarily released for a period not exceeding fifteen days where, in his opinion, it is necessary or desirable that the young person be absent, with or without escort, for medical, compassionate or humanitarian reasons or for the purpose of rehabilitating the young person or re-integrating him into the community; or
      (*b*) to be released from custody on such days and during such hours as he specifies in order that the young person may
         (i) attend school or any other educational or training institution,
         (ii) obtain or continue employment or perform domestic or other duties required by the young person's family,
         (iii) participate in a program specified by him that, in his opinion, will enable the young person to better carry out his employment or improve his education or training, or
         (iv) attend an out-patient treatment program or other program that provides services that are suitable to addressing the young person's needs.
   (2) A young person who is released from custody pursuant to subsection (1) shall be released only for such periods of time as are necessary to attain the purpose for which the young person is released.
   (3) The provincial director of a province may, at any time, revoke an authorization made under subsection (1).

(4) Where the provincial director revokes an authorization for a young person to be released from custody under subsection (3) or where a young person fails to comply with any term or condition of release from custody under this section, the young person may be arrested without warrant and returned to custody.

(5) A young person who has been committed to custody under this Act shall not be released from custody before the expiration of the period of his custody except in accordance with subsection (1) unless the release is ordered under sections 28 to 31 or otherwise according to law by a court of competent jurisdiction. R.S. 1985, c.24 (2d Supp.), s.26; c.1 (4th Supp.), s.42; 1995, c.19, s.25.

EFFECT OF TERMINATION OF DISPOSITION

Effect of absolute discharge or termination of dispositions — Disqualifications removed — Applications for employment — Punishment — Finding of guilt not a previous conviction.

36. (1) Subject to section 12 of the Canada Evidence Act, where a young person is found guilty of an offence, and

(*a*) a youth court directs under paragraph 20(1)(*a*) that the young person be discharged absolutely, or

(*b*) all the dispositions made under this Act in respect of the offence, and all terms of those dispositions, have ceased to have effect,

(*b*) all the dispositions made under subsection 20(1) in respect of the offence have ceased to have effect, 1995, c. 39, s. 183. Not in force at date of publication.

Conditional Amendment

When 1995, c. 39, s. 179, is proclaimed, paragraph 36(1)(b) of the *Young Offenders Act* is replaced with following:

(*b*) all the dispositions made under subsection 20(1) in respect of the offence, and all terms of those dispositions, have ceased to have effect.
1995, c. 39, s. 189(*a*). Not in force at date of publication.

the young person shall be deemed not to have been found guilty or convicted of the offence except that,

(*c*) the young person may plead autrefois convict in respect of any subsequent charge relating to the offence;

(*d*) a youth court may consider the finding of guilt in considering an application for a transfer to ordinary court under section 16;

(*e*) any court or justice may consider the finding of guilt in considering an application for judicial interim release or in considering what dispositions to make or sentence to impose for any offence; and

(*f*) the National Parole Board or any provincial parole board may consider the finding of guilt in considering an application for parole or pardon.

(2) For greater certainty and without restricting the generality of subsection (1), an absolute discharge under paragraph 20(1)(*a*) or the termination of all dispositions in respect of an offence for which a young person is found guilty removes any disqualification in respect of the offence to which the young person is subject pursuant to any Act of Parliament by reason of a conviction.

(3) No application form for or relating to

(*a*) employment in any department, as defined in section 2 of the Financial Administration Act,

(*b*) employment by any Crown corporation as defined in section 83 of the Financial Administration Act,

(*c*) enrolment in the Canadian Forces, or

(*d*) employment on or in connection with the operation of any work, undertaking or business that is within the legislative authority of Parliament,

shall contain any question that by its terms requires the applicant to disclose that he has been charged with or found guilty of an offence in respect of which he has, under this Act, been discharged absolutely or has completed all the dispositions.

shall contain any question that by its terms requires the applicant to disclose that the applicant has been charged with or found guilty of an offence in respect of which the applicant has, under this Act, been discharged absolutely or has completed all the dispositions made under subsection 20(1). 1995, c. 39, s. 183(2). Not in force at date of publication.

(4) Any person who uses or authorizes the use of an application form in contravention of subsection (3) is guilty of an offence punishable on summary conviction.

(5) A finding of guilt under this Act is not a previous conviction for the purposes of any offence under any Act of Parliament for which a greater punishment is prescribed by reason of previous convictions. R.S. 1985, c. 24 (2d Supp.), s. 27; 1995, c. 19, s. 26.

YOUTH WORKERS

Duties of youth worker.
37. The duties and functions of a youth worker in respect of a young person whose case has been assigned to him by the provincial director include

(*a*) where the young person is bound by a probation order that requires him to be under supervision, supervising the young person in complying with the conditions of the probation order or in carrying out any other disposition made together with it;

(*a*.1) where the young person is placed under conditional supervision pursuant to an order made under section 26.2, supervising the young person in complying with the conditions of the order;

(*b*) where the young person is found guilty of any offence, giving such assistance to him as he considers appropriate up to the time the young person is discharged or the disposition of his case terminates;

(*c*) attending court when he considers it advisable or when required by the youth court to be present;

(*d*) preparing, at the request of the provincial director, a pre-disposition report or a progress report; and

(*e*) performing such other duties and functions as the provincial director requires. R.S. 1985, c. 24 (2d Supp.), s. 28; 1992, c. 11, s. 13.

PROTECTION OF PRIVACY OF YOUNG PERSONS

Identity not to be published — Limitation — Preparation of reports — No subsequent disclosure — Schools and others — No subsequent disclosure — Information to be kept separate — Ex parte application for leave to publish — Order ceases to have effect — Application for leave to publish — Disclosure with court order — Opportunity to be heard — Ex parte application — Time limit — Contravention — Provincial court judge has absolute jurisdiction on indictment.

38. (1) Subject to this section, no person shall publish by any means any report

(*a*) of an offence committed or alleged to have been committed by a young person, unless an order has been made under section 16 with respect thereto, or

(*b*) of any hearing, adjudication, disposition or appeal concerning a young person who committed or is alleged to have committed an offence

in which the name of the young person, a child or a young person who is a victim of the offence or a child or a young person who appeared as a witness in connection with the offence, or in which any information serving to identify the young person or child, is disclosed.

(1.1) Subsection (1) does not apply in respect of the disclosure of information in the course of the administration of justice where it is not the purpose of the disclosure to make the information known in the community.

(1.1) Subsection (1) does no apply in respect of the disclosure of information in the course of administration of justice including, for greater certainty, the disclosure of information for the purposes of the Firearms Act and Part III of the Criminal Code, where it is not the purpose of the disclosure to make the information known in the community. 1995, c. 39, s. 184. Not in force at date of publication.

(1.11) Subsection (1) does not apply in respect of the disclosure of information by the provincial director or a youth worker where the disclosure is necessary for procuring information that relates to the preparation of any report required by this Act.

(1.12) No person to whom information is disclosed pursuant to subsection (1.11) shall disclose that information to any other person unless the disclosure is necessary for the purpose of preparing the report for which the information was disclosed.

(1.13) Subsection (1) does not apply in respect of the disclosure of information to any professional or other person engaged in the supervision or care of a young person, including the representative of any school board or school or any other educational or training institution, by the provincial director, a youth worker, a peace officer or any other person engaged in the provision of services to young persons where the disclosure is necessary

 (*a*) to ensure compliance by the young person with an authorization pursuant to section 35 or an order of any court concerning bail, probation or conditional supervision; or

 (*b*) to ensure the safety of staff, students or other persons, as the case may be.

(1.14) No person to whom information is disclosed pursuant to subsection (1.13) shall disclose that information to any other person unless the disclosure is necessary for a purpose referred to in that subsection.

(1.15) Any person to whom information is disclosed pursuant to subsections (1.13) and (1.14) shall

 (*a*) keep the information separate from any other record of the young person to whom the information relates;

 (*b*) subject to subsection (1.14), ensure that no other person has access to the information; and

 (*c*) destroy the information when the information is no longer required for the purpose for which it was disclosed.

(1.2) A youth court judge shall, on the ex parte application of a peace officer, make an order permitting any person to publish a report described in subsection (1) that contains the name of a young person, or information serving to identify a young person, who has committed or is alleged to have committed an indictable offence, if the judge is satisfied that

 (*a*) there is reason to believe that the young person is dangerous to others; and

 (*b*) publication of the report is necessary to assist in apprehending the young person.

(1.3) An order made under subsection (1.2) shall cease to have effect two days after it is made.

(1.4) The youth court may, on the application of any person referred to in subsection (1), make an order permitting any person to publish a report in which the name of that person, or information serving to identify that person, would be disclosed, if the court is satisfied that the publication of the report would not be contrary to the best interests of that person.

(1.5) The youth court may, on the application of the provincial director, the Attorney General or an agent of the Attorney General or a peace officer, make an order permitting the applicant to disclose to such person or persons as are specified by the court such information about a young person as is specified if the court is satisfied that the disclosure is necessary, having regard to the following:

 (*a*) the young person has been found guilty of an offence involving serious personal injury;

 (*b*) the young person poses a risk of serious harm to persons; and

 (*c*) the disclosure of the information is relevant to the avoidance of that risk.

(1.6) Subject to subsection (1.7), before making an order under subsection (1.5), the youth court shall afford the young person, the young person's parents, the Attorney General or an agent of the Attorney General an opportunity to be heard.

(1.7) An application under subsection (1.5) may be made ex parte by the Attorney General or an agent of the Attorney General where the youth court is satisfied that reasonable efforts have been made to locate the young person and that those efforts have not been successful.

(1.8) No information may be disclosed pursuant to subsection (1.5) after the record to which the information relates ceases to be available for inspection under subsection 45(1).

(2) Every one who contravenes subsection (1), (1.12), (1.14) or (1.15)

 (*a*) is guilty of an indictable offence and liable to imprisonment for a term not exceeding two years; or

 (*b*) is guilty of an offence punishable on summary conviction.

(3) Where an accused is charged with an offence under paragraph (2)(*a*), a provincial court judge has absolute jurisdiction to try the case and his jurisdiction does not depend on the consent of the accused. R.S. 1985, c. 27 (1st Supp.), s. 203; c. 24 (2d Supp.), s. 29; 1995, c. 19, s. 27.

Exclusion from hearing — Exception — Exclusion after adjudication or during review — Exception.

39. (1) Subject to subsection (2), where a court or justice before whom proceedings are carried out under this Act is of the opinion

(*a*) that any evidence or information presented to the court or justice would be seriously injurious or seriously prejudicial to

(i) the young person who is being dealt with in the proceedings,

(ii) a child or young person who is a witness in the proceedings,

(iii) a child or young person who is aggrieved by or the victim of the offence charged in the proceedings, or

(*b*) that it would be in the interest of public morals, the maintenance of order or the proper administration of justice to exclude any or all members of the public from the court room,

the court or justice may exclude any person from all or part of the proceedings if the court or justice deems that person's presence to be unnecessary to the conduct of the proceedings.

(2) Subject to section 650 of the Criminal Code and except where it is necessary for the purposes of subsection 13(6) of this Act, a court or justice may not, pursuant to subsection (1), exclude from proceedings under this Act

(*a*) the prosecutor;

(*b*) the young person who is being dealt with in the proceedings, his parent, his counsel or any adult assisting him pursuant to subsection 11(7);

(*c*) the provincial director or his agent;

(*d*) the youth worker to whom the young person's case has been assigned.

(3) The youth court, after it has found a young person guilty of an offence, or the youth court or the review board, during a review of a disposition under sections 28 to 32, may, in its discretion, exclude from the court or from a hearing of the review board, as the case may be, any person other than

(*a*) the young person or his counsel,

(*b*) the provincial director or his agent,

(*c*) the youth worker to whom the young person's case has been assigned, and

(*d*) the Attorney General or his agent,

when any information is being presented to the court or the review board the knowledge of which might, in the opinion of the court or review board, be seriously injurious or seriously prejudicial to the young person.

(4) The exception set out in paragraph (3)(*a*) is subject to subsection 13(6) of this Act and section 650 of the Criminal Code. R.S. 1985, c. 24 (2d Supp.), s. 30.

MAINTENANCE AND USE OF RECORDS
Records that may be Kept

Youth court, review board and other courts — Exception.

40. (1) A youth court, review board or any court dealing with matters arising out of proceedings under this Act may keep a record of any case arising under this Act that comes before it.

(2) For greater certainty, this section does not apply in respect of proceedings held in ordinary court pursuant to an order under section 16.

(3) *Records of offences that result in order under s. 20.1* — Notwithstanding anything in this Act, where a young person is found guilty of an offence that results in an order under section 20.1 being made against the young person, the youth court may keep a record of the conviction and the order until the expiration of the order.

(4) *Disclosure* — Any record that is kept under subsection (3) may be disclosed only to establish the existence of the order in any offence involving a breach of the order. 1995, c. 39, s. 185. Not in force at date of publication.

R.S. 1985, c. 24 (2d Supp.), s. 31.

Records in central repository — Police force may provide record — Police force shall provide record.

41. (1) A record of any offence that a young person has been charged with having committed may, where the offence is an offence in respect of which an adult may be subjected to any measurement, process or operation referred to in the Identification of Criminals Act, be kept in such central repository as the Commissioner of the Royal Canadian Mounted Police may, from time to time, designate for the purpose of keeping criminal history files or records on offenders or keeping records for the identification of offenders.

(2) Where a young person is charged with having committed an offence referred to in subsection (1), the police force responsible for the investigation of the offence may provide a record of the offence, including the original or a copy of any fingerprints, palmprints or photographs and any other measurement, process or operation referred to in the Identification of Criminals Act taken of, or applied in respect of, the young person by or on behalf of the police force, for inclusion in any central repository designated pursuant to subsection (1).

(3) Where a young person is found guilty of an offence referred to in subsection (1), the police force responsible for the investigation of the offence shall provide a record of the offence, including the original or a copy of any fingerprints, palmprints or photographs and any other measurement, process or operation referred to in the Identification of Criminals Act taken of, or applied in respect of, the young person by or on behalf of the police force, for inclusion in any central repository designated pursuant to subsection (1). R.S. 1985, c. 24 (2d Supp.), s. 31; 1995, c. 19, s. 28.

Police records.
42. A record relating to any offence alleged to have been committed by a young person, including the original or a copy of any fingerprints or photographs of the young person, may be kept by any police force responsible for, or participating in, the investigation of the offence.

(2)–(5) [Repealed R.S. 1985, c. 24 (2d Supp.), s. 31.]
R.S. 1985, c. 24 (2d Supp.), s. 31.

Government records — Private records.
43. (1) A department or agency of any government in Canada may keep records containing information obtained by the department or agency
(*a*) for the purposes of an investigation of an offence alleged to have been committed by a young person;
(*b*) for use in proceedings against a young person under this Act;
(*c*) for the purpose of administering a disposition;
(*d*) for the purpose of considering whether, instead of commencing or continuing judicial proceedings under this Act against a young person, to use alternative measures to deal with the young person; or
(*e*) as a result of the use of alternative measures to deal with a young person.

(2) Any person or organization may keep records containing information obtained by the person or organization
(*a*) as a result of the use of alternative measures to deal with a young person alleged to have committed an offence; or
(*b*) for the purpose of administering or participating in the administration of a disposition.

(3), (4) [Repealed R.S. 1985, c. 24 (2d Supp.), s. 32.]

Fingerprints and Photographs

Identification of Criminals Act applies — Limitation.
44. (1) Subject to this section, the Identification of Criminals Act applies in respect of young persons.

(2) No fingerprints, palmprints or photograph or any other measurement, process or operation referred to in the Identification of Criminals Act shall be taken of, or applied in respect of, a young person who is charged with having committed an offence except in the circumstances in which an adult may, under that Act, be subjected to the measurements, processes and operations referred to in that Act.

(3)–(5) [Repealed R.S. 1985, c. 24 (2d Supp.), s. 33.]
1995, c. 19, s. 29.

Disclosure of Records

Records made available — Exception — Records of forensic DNA analysis of bodily sub-

stances — Introduction into evidence — Disclosures for research or statistical purposes — Record made available to victim — Disclosure of information and copies of records.

44.1 (1) Subject to subsections (2), (2.1), any record that is kept pursuant to section 40 shall, and any record that is kept pursuant to sections 41 to 43 may, on request, be made available for inspection to

(a) the young person to whom the record relates;

(b) counsel acting on behalf of the young person, or any representative of that counsel;

(c) the Attorney General or his agent;

(d) a parent of the young person or any adult assisting the young person pursuant to subsection 11(7), during the course of any proceedings relating to the offence or alleged offence to which the record relates or during the term of any disposition made in respect of the offence;

(e) any judge, court or review board, for any purpose relating to proceedings relating to the young person under this Act or to proceedings in ordinary court in respect of offences committed or alleged to have been committed by the young person, whether as a young person or an adult;

(f) any peace officer,

(i) for the purpose of investigating any offence that the young person is suspected on reasonable grounds of having committed, or in respect of which the young person has been arrested or charged, whether as a young person or an adult,

(ii) for any purpose related to the administration of the case to which the record relates during the course of proceedings against the young person or the term of any disposition, or

(iii) for the purpose of investigating any offence that another person is suspected on reasonable grounds of having committed against the young person while the young person is, or was, serving a disposition, or

(iv) for any other law enforcement purpose;

(g) any member of a department or agency of a government in Canada, or any agent thereof, that is

(i) engaged in the administration of alternative measures in respect of the young person,

(ii) preparing a report in respect of the young person pursuant to this Act or for the purpose of assisting a court in sentencing the young person after he becomes an adult or is transferred to ordinary court pursuant to section 16,

(iii) engaged in the supervision or care of the young person, whether as a young person or an adult, or in the administration of a disposition or a sentence in respect of the young person, whether as a young person or an adult, or

(iv) considering an application for parole or pardon made by the young person after he becomes an adult;

(h) any person, or person within a class of persons, designated by the Governor in Council, or the Lieutenant Governor in Council of a province, for a purpose and to the extent specified by the Governor in Council or the Lieutenant Governor in Council, as the case may be;

(i) any person, for the purpose of determining whether to grant security clearances required by the Government of Canada or the government of a province or a municipality for purposes of employment or the performance of services;

(i.1) to any person for the purposes of the Firearms Act;
1995, c. 39, s. 186. Not in force at date of publication.

(j) any employee or agent of the Government of Canada, for statistical purposes pursuant to the Statistics Act; and

(k) any other person who is deemed, or any person within a class of persons that is deemed, by a youth court judge to have a valid interest in the record, to the extent directed by the judge, if the judge is satisfied that the disclosure is

(i) desirable in the public interest for research or statistical purposes, or

(ii) desirable in the interest of the proper administration of justice.

(2) Where a youth court has withheld the whole or a part of a report from any person pursuant to subsection 13(6) or 14(7), the report or part thereof shall not be made available to that person for inspection under subsection (1).

(2.1) Notwithstanding subsections (1) and (5), any record that is kept pursuant to any of sections 40 to 43 and that is a record of the results of forensic DNA analysis of a bodily substance taken from a young person in execution of a warrant issued under section 487.05 of the Criminal Code may be made available for inspection under this section only under paragraphs (1)(*a*), (*b*), (*c*), (*d*), (*e*), (*f*), (*h*) or subparagraph (1)(*k*)(ii).

(3) Nothing in paragraph (1)(*e*) authorizes the introduction into evidence of any part of a record that would not otherwise be admissible in evidence.

(4) Where a record is made available for inspection to any person under paragraph (1)(*j*) or subparagraph (1)(*k*)(i), that person may subsequently disclose information contained in the record, but may not disclose the information in any form that would reasonably be expected to identify the young person to whom it relates.

(5) Any record that is kept pursuant to sections 40 to 43 may, on request, be made available for inspection to the victim of the offence to which the record relates.

(6) Any person to whom a record is required or authorized to be made available for inspection under this section may be given any information contained in the record and may be given a copy of any part of the record. R.S. 1985, c. 24 (2d Supp.), s. 34; 1992, c. 43, s. 34; 1995, c. 27, s. 2; 1995, c. 19, s. 30.

Disclosure by peace officer during investigation — Disclosure to insurance company.

44.2 (1) A peace officer may disclose to any person any information in a record kept pursuant to section 42 that it is necessary to disclose in the conduct of the investigation of an offence.

(2) A peace officer may disclose to an insurance company information in any record that is kept pursuant to section 42 for the purpose of investigating any claim arising out of an offence committed or alleged to have been committed by the young person to whom the record relates. R.S. 1985, c. 24 (2d Supp.), s. 34.

Non-disclosure and Destruction of Records

Non-disclosure — Destruction of record — Transfer of records relating to serious offences — Transfer of fingerprints — Meaning of "destroy" Other records may be destroyed — Young person deemed not to have committed offence — Deemed election — Application to delinquency.

45. (1) Subject to sections 45.01, 45.1 and 45.2, records kept pursuant to sections 40 to 43 may not be made available for inspection under section 44.1 or 44.2 in the following circumstances:

(*a*) where the young person to whom the record relates is charged with the offence to which the record relates and is acquitted otherwise than by reason of a verdict of not criminally responsible on account of mental disorder, on the expiration of two months after the expiration of the time allowed for the taking of an appeal or, where an appeal is taken on the expiration of three months after all proceedings in respect of the appeal have been completed;

(*b*) where the charge against the young person is dismissed for any reason other than acquittal or withdrawn, on the expiration of one year after the dismissal or withdrawal;

(*c*) where the charge against the young person is stayed, with no proceedings being taken against the young person for a period of one year, on the expiration of the one year;

(*d*) where alternative measures are used to deal with the young person, on the expiration of two years after the young person consents to participate in the alternative measures in accordance with paragraph 4(1)(*c*);

(*d.1*) where the young person is found guilty of the offence and the disposition is an absolute discharge, on the expiration of one year after the young person is found guilty;

(*d.2*) where the young person is found guilty of the offence and the disposition is a conditional discharge, on the expiration of three years after the young person is found guilty;

(*e*) subject to paragraph (*g*), where the young person is found guilty of the offence and it is a summary conviction offence, on the expiration of three years after all dispositions made in respect of that offence;

(*f*) subject to paragraph (*g*), where the young person is found guilty of the offence and it is an indictable offence, on the expiration of five years after all dispositions made in respect of that offence; and

(*g*) where, before the expiration of the period referred to in paragraph (*e*) or (*f*), the young person is, as a young person, found guilty of

(i) a subsequent summary conviction offence, on the expiration of three years after all dispositions made in respect of that offence have been completed, and

(ii) a subsequent indictable offence, five years after all dispositions made in respect of that offence have been completed. 1995, c. 19, s. 31(2), (4). Not in force at date of publication.

[Note: 1995, c. 19, s. 31(4) states: Paragraphs 45(1)(d.1) to (e) of the Act, as enacted by subsection (2), apply in respect of a record relating to a finding of guilt made before the coming into force of that subsection only if the person to whom the record relates applies, after the coming into force of that subsection, to the Royal Canadian Mounted Police to have those paragraphs apply.]

(2) Subject to subsections (2.1) and (2.2), when the circumstances set out in subsection (1) are realized in respect of any record kept pursuant to section 41, the record shall be destroyed forthwith.

(2.1) Where a special records repository has been established pursuant to subsection 45.02(1), all records in the central repository referred to in subsection 41(1) that relate to a conviction for first degree murder or second degree murder within the meaning of section 231 of the *Criminal Code* or an offence referred to in the schedule shall, when the circumstances set out in subsection (1) are realized in respect of the records, be transferred to that special records repository.

Conditional Amendment

When 1995, c. 39, s. 185 is proclaimed, subsection 45(2.1) of the *Young Offenders Act* is replaced with the following:

(2.1) *Transfer of records relating to serious offences* — Where a special records repository has been established pursuant to subsection 45.02(1), all records in the central repository referred to in subsection 41(1) that relate to

(*a*) a conviction for first degree murder or second degree murder within the meaning of section 231 of the Criminal Code,

(*b*) an offence referred to in the schedule, or

(*c*) an order made under section 20.1,

shall, when the circumstances set out in subsection (1) are realized in respect of the records, be transferred to that special records repository.

1995, c. 39, s. 189(*b*). Not in force at date of publication.

(2.2) Where a special fingerprints repository has been established pursuant to subsection 45.03(1), all fingerprints and any information necessary to identify the person to whom the fingerprints belong that are in the central repository referred to in subsection 41(1) shall, when the circumstances set out in subsection (1) are realized in respect of the records, be transferred to that special fingerprints repository.

(2.3) For the purposes of subsection (2), "destroy", in respect of a record, means

(*a*) to shred, burn or otherwise physically destroy the record, in the case of a record other than a record in electronic form; and

(*b*) to delete, write over or otherwise render the record inaccessible, in the case of a record in electronic form.

(3) Any record kept pursuant to sections 40 to 43 may, in the discretion of the person or body keeping the record, be destroyed at any time before or after the circumstances set out in subsection (1) are realized in respect of that record.

(4) A young person shall be deemed not to have committed any offence to which a record kept pursuant to sections 40 to 43 relates when the circumstances set out in paragraph (1)(*d*), (*e*) or (*f*) are realized in respect of that record.

(5) For the purposes of paragraphs (1)(*e*) and (*f*), where no election is made in respect of an offence that may be prosecuted by indictment or proceeded with by way of summary conviction, the Attorney General or his agent shall be deemed to have elected to proceed with the offence as an offence punishable on summary conviction.

(5.1) For the purposes of this Act, orders made under section 20.1 shall not be taken into account in determining any time period referred to in subsection (1). 1995, c. 39, s. 187. Not in force at date of publication.

(6) This section applies, with such modifications as the circumstances require, in respect of records relating to the offence of delinquency under the Juvenile Delinquents Act, chapter J-3 of the Revised Statutes of Canada, 1970, as it read immediately prior to April 2, 1984. R.S. 1985, c. 24 (2d Supp.), s. 35; 1992, c. 43, s. 34; 1995, c. 19, s. 31.

Retention of Records

Retention of records.
45.01 Where, before the expiration of the period referred to in paragraph 45(1)(*e*) or (*f*) or subparagraph 45(1)(*g*)(i) or (ii), the young person is found guilty of a subsequent offence as an adult, records kept pursuant to sections 40 to 43 shall be available for inspection under section 44.1 or 44.2 and the provisions applicable to criminal records of adults shall apply. 1995, c. 19, s. 32.

Special Records Repository

Special records repository — Records relating to murder — Records relating to other serious offences — Disclosure.
45.02 (1) The Commissioner of the Royal Canadian Mounted Police may establish a special records repository for records transferred pursuant to subsection 45(2.1).

(2) A record that relates to a conviction for the offence of first degree murder or second degree murder within the meaning of section 231 of the *Criminal Code* or an offence referred to in any of paragraphs 16(1.01)(*b*) to (*d*) may be kept indefinitely in the special records repository.

(3) A record that relates to a conviction for an offence referred to in the schedule shall be kept in the special records repository for a period of five years and shall be destroyed forthwith at the expiration of that five year period, unless the young person to whom the record relates is subsequently found guilty of any offence referred to in the schedule, in which case the record shall be dealt with as the record of an adult.

(4) A record kept in the special records repository shall be made available for inspection to the following persons at the following times or in the following circumstances:
(*a*) at any time, to the person to whom the record relates and to counsel acting on behalf of the young person, or any representative of that counsel;
(*b*) where the young person has subsequently been charged with the commission of first degree murder or second degree murder within the meaning of section 231 of the *Criminal Code* or an offence referred to in the schedule, to any peace officer for the purpose of investigating any offence that the young person is suspected of having committed, or in respect of which the young person has been arrested or charged, whether as a young person or as an adult;
(*c*) where the young person has subsequently been convicted of an offence referred to in the schedule,
(i) to the Attorney General or an agent of the Attorney General,
(ii) to a parent of the young person or any adult assisting the young person,
(iii) to any judge, court or review board, for any purpose relating to proceedings relating to the young person under this Act or to proceedings in ordinary court in respect of offences committed or alleged to have been committed by the young person, whether as a young person or as an adult, or
(iv) to any member of a department or agency of a government in Canada, or any agent thereof, that is
(A) engaged in the administration of alternative measures in respect of the young person,
(B) preparing a report in respect of the young person pursuant to this Act or for the purpose of assisting a court in sentencing the young person after the

young person becomes an adult or is transferred to ordinary court pursuant to section 16,

(C) engaged in the supervision or care of the young person, whether as a young person or as an adult, or in the administration of a disposition or a sentence in respect of the young person, whether as a young person or as an adult, or

(D) considering an application for parole or pardon made by the young person after the young person becomes an adult;

Conditional Amendment

When 1995, c. 39, s. 185 is proclaimed subsection 45.02(4) of the *Young Offenders Act* is amended by adding the following after paragraph 45.02(4)(c):

(c.1) to establish the existence of the order in any offence involving a breach of the order;

(c.2) for the purposes of the Firearms Act;

1995, c. 39, s. 189(d). Not in force at date of publication.

(d) at any time, to any employee or agent of the Government of Canada, for statistical purposes pursuant to the Statistics Act; or

(e) at any time, to any other person who is deemed, or any person within a class of persons that is deemed, by a youth court judge to have a valid interest in the record, to the extent directed by the judge, if the judge is satisfied that the disclosure is desirable in the public interest for research or statistical purposes. 1995, c. 19, s. 32.

Special Fingerprints Repository

Special fingerprints repository — Disclosure for identification purposes — Destruction.

45.03 (1) The Commissioner of the Royal Canadian Mounted Police may establish a special fingerprints repository for fingerprints and any related information transferred pursuant to subsection 45(2.2).

(2) Fingerprints and any related information may be kept in the special fingerprints repository for a period of five years following the date of their receipt and, during that time, the name, date of birth and last known address of the young person to whom the fingerprints belong may be disclosed for identification purposes if a fingerprint identified as that of the young person is found during the investigation of a crime or during an attempt to identify a deceased person or a person suffering from amnesia.

(3) Fingerprints and any related information in the special fingerprints repository shall be destroyed five years after the date of their receipt in the repository.

1995, c. 19, s. 32.

Conditional Amendment

When 1995, c. 39, s. 185 is proclaimed, section 45.03 of the *Young Offenders Act* is amended by adding the following after subsection 45.03(3):

(3.1) *Records of orders made under s. 20.1* — A record that relates to an order made under section 20.1 shall be kept in the special records repository until the expiration of the order and shall be destroyed forthwith at that time.

1995, c. 39, s. 189(c). Not in force at date of publication.

Disclosure in Special Circumstances

Where records may be made available — Notice — Records — Notice — Where notice not required — Use of record.

45.1 (1) Subject to subsection (1.1), a youth court judge may, on application by any person, order that any record to which subsection 45(1) applies, or any part thereof, be made available for inspection to that person or a copy of the record or part thereof be given to that person, if a youth court judge is satisfied that

(a) that person has a valid and substantial interest in the record or part thereof;

(b) it is necessary for the record, part thereof or copy thereof to be made available in the interest of the proper administration of justice; and

(c) disclosure of the record or part thereof or information is not prohibited under any other Act of Parliament or the legislature of a province.

(2) An application under subsection (1) in respect of a record shall not be heard unless the person who makes the application has given the young person to whom the record relates and the person or body that has possession of the record at least five days notice in writing of the application and the young person and the person or body that has possession has had a reasonable opportunity to be heard.

(1.1) Subsection (1) applies in respect of any record relating to a particular young person or to any record relating to a class of young persons where the identity of young persons in the class at the time of the making of the application referred to in that subsection cannot reasonably be ascertained and the disclosure of the record is necessary for the purpose of investigating any offence that a person is suspected on reasonable grounds of having committed against a young person while the young person is, or was, serving a disposition.

(2) Subject to subsection (2.1), an application under subsection (1) in respect of a record shall not be heard unless the person who makes the application has given the young person to whom the record relates and the person or body that has possession of the record at least five days notice in writing of the application and the young person and the person or body that has possession has had a reasonable opportunity to be heard.

(2.1) A youth court judge may waive the requirement in subsection (2) to give notice to a young person where the youth court is of the opinion that
(a) to insist on the giving of the notice would frustrate the application; or
(b) reasonable efforts have not been successful in finding the young person.

(3) In any order under subsection (1), the youth court judge shall set out the purposes for which the record may be used. R.S. 1985, c. 24 (2d Supp.), s. 35; 1995, c. 19, s. 34.

Records in the custody, etc. of archivists.

45.2 Where records originally kept pursuant to section 40, 42 or 43 are under the custody or control of the National Archivist of Canada or the archivist for any province, that person may disclose any information contained in the records to any other person if
(a) the Attorney General or his agent is satisfied that the disclosure is desirable in the public interest for research or statistical purposes; and
(b) the person to whom the information is disclosed undertakes not to disclose the information in any form that could reasonably be expected to identify the young person to whom it relates. R.S. 1985, c. 24 (2d Supp.), s. 35; c. 1 (3d Supp.), s. 12.

Prohibition against disclosure — Exception for employees — Prohibition against use — Offence — Absolute jurisdiction of provincial court judge.

46. (1) Except as authorized or required by this Act, no record kept pursuant to sections 40 to 43 may be made available for inspection, and no copy, print or negative thereof or information contained therein may be given, to any person where to do so would serve to identify the young person to whom it relates as a young person dealt with under this Act.

(2) No person who is employed in keeping or maintaining records referred to in subsection (1) is restricted from doing anything prohibited under subsection (1) with respect to any other person so employed.

(3) Subject to section 45.1, no record kept pursuant to sections 40 to 43, and no copy, print or negative thereof, may be used for any purpose that would serve to identify the young person to whom the record relates as a young person dealt with under this Act after the circumstances set out in subsection 45(1) are realized in respect of that record.

(4) Any person who fails to comply with this section or subsection 45(2)
(a) is guilty of an indictable offence and liable to imprisonment for a term not exceeding two years; or
(b) is guilty of an offence punishable on summary conviction.

(5) The jurisdiction of a provincial court judge to try an accused is absolute and does not depend on the consent of the accused where the accused is charged with an offence under paragraph (4)(a). R.S. 1985, c. 27 (1st Supp.), s. 203; c. 24 (2d Supp.), s. 36.

CONTEMPT OF COURT

Contempt against youth court — Exclusive jurisdiction of youth court — Concurrent jurisdiction of youth court — Dispositions — Section 708 of Criminal Code applies in respect of adults — Appeals.

47. (1) Every youth court has the same power, jurisdiction and authority to deal with and impose punishment for contempt against the court as may be exercised by the superior court of criminal jurisdiction of the province in which the court is situated.

(2) The youth court has exclusive jurisdiction in respect of every contempt of court committed by a young person against the youth court whether or not committed in the face of the court and every contempt of court committed by a young person against any other court otherwise than in the face of that court.

(3) The youth court has jurisdiction in respect of every contempt of court committed by a young person against any other court in the face of that court and every contempt of court committed by an adult against the youth court in the face of the youth court, but nothing in this subsection affects the power, jurisdiction or authority of any other court to deal with or impose punishment for contempt of court.

(4) Where a youth court or any other court finds a young person guilty of contempt of court, it may make any one of the dispositions set out in section 20, or any number thereof that are not inconsistent with each other, but no other disposition or sentence.

(5) Section 708 of the *Criminal Code* applies in respect of proceedings under this section in youth court against adults, with such modifications as the circumstances require.

(6) A finding of guilt under this section for contempt of court or a disposition or sentence made in respect thereof may be appealed as if the finding were a conviction or the disposition or sentence were a sentence in a prosecution by indictment in ordinary court.

FORFEITURE OF RECOGNIZANCES

Applications for forfeiture of recognizances.
48. Applications for the forfeiture of recognizances of young persons shall be made to the youth court.

Proceedings in case of default — Order for forfeiture of recognizance — Judgment debtors of the Crown — Order may be filed — Where a deposit has been made — Subsections 770(2) and (4) of Criminal Code do not apply — Sections 772 and 773 of Criminal Code apply.
49. (1) Where a recognizance binding a young person has been endorsed with a certificate pursuant to subsection 770(1) of the *Criminal Code*, a youth court judge shall,

(*a*) on the request of the Attorney General or his agent, fix a time and place for the hearing of an application for the forfeiture of the recognizance; and

(*b*) after fixing a time and place for the hearing, cause to be sent by registered mail, not less than ten days before the time so fixed, to each principal and surety named in the recognizance, directed to him at his latest known address, a notice requiring him to appear at the time and place fixed by the judge to show cause why the recognizance should not be forfeited.

(2) Where subsection (1) is complied with, the youth court judge may, after giving the parties an opportunity to be heard, in his discretion grant or refuse the application and make any order with respect to the forfeiture of the recognizance that he considers proper.

(3) Where, pursuant to subsection (2), a youth court judge orders forfeiture of a recognizance, the principal and his sureties become judgment debtors of the Crown, each in the amount that the judge orders him to pay.

(4) An order made under subsection (2) may be filed with the clerk of the superior court or, in the province of Quebec, the prothonotary and, where an order is filed, the clerk or the prothonotary shall issue a writ of *fieri facias* in Form 34 set out in the *Criminal Code* and deliver it to the sheriff of each of the territorial divisions in which any of the principal and his sureties resides, carries on business or has property.

(5) Where a deposit has been made by a person against whom an order for forfeiture of a recognizance has been made, no writ of *fieri facias* shall issue, but the amount of the deposit shall be transferred by the person who has custody of it to the person who is entitled by law to receive it.

(6) Subsections 770(2) and (4) of the *Criminal Code* do not apply in respect of proceedings under this Act.

(7) Sections 772 and 773 of the *Criminal Code* apply in respect of writs of *fieri facias* issued pursuant to this section as if they were issued pursuant to section 771 of the *Criminal Code*.

INTERFERENCE WITH DISPOSITIONS

Inducing a young person, etc. — Absolute jurisdiction of provincial court judge.

50. (1) Every one who

(*a*) induces or assists a young person to leave unlawfully a place of custody or other place in which the young person has been placed pursuant to a disposition,

(*b*) unlawfully removes a young person from a place referred to in paragraph (*a*),

(*c*) knowingly harbours or conceals a young person who has unlawfully left a place referred to in paragraph (*a*),

(*d*) wilfully induces or assists a young person to breach or disobey a term or condition of a disposition, or

(*e*) wilfully prevents or interferes with the performance by a young person of a term or condition of a disposition

is guilty of an indictable offence and liable to imprisonment for a term not exceeding two years or is guilty of an offence punishable on summary conviction.

(2) The jurisdiction of a provincial court judge to try an adult accused of an indictable offence under this section is absolute and does not depend on the consent of the accused. R.S. 1985, c. 27 (1st Supp.), s. 203; c. 24 (2d Supp.), s. 37.

APPLICATION OF THE CRIMINAL CODE

Application of Criminal Code.

51. Except to the extent that they are inconsistent with or excluded by this Act, all the provisions of the *Criminal Code* apply, with such modifications as the circumstances require, in respect of offences alleged to have been committed by young persons.

PROCEDURE

Part XXVII and summary conviction trial provisions of Criminal Code to apply — Indictable offences — Attendance of young person — Limitation period — Costs.

52. (1) Subject to this section and except to the extent that they are inconsistent with this Act,

(*a*) the provisions of Part XXVII of the *Criminal Code*, and

(*b*) any other provisions of the *Criminal Code that apply in respect of summary conviction offences and relate to trial proceedings*

apply to proceedings under this Act

(*c*) in respect of a summary conviction offence, and

(*d*) in respect of an indictable offence as if it were defined in the enactment creating it as a summary conviction offence.

(2) For greater certainty and notwithstanding subsection (1) or any other provision of this Act, an indictable offence committed by a young person is, for the purposes of this or any other Act, an indictable offence.

(3) Section 650 of the *Criminal Code* applies in respect of proceedings under this Act, whether the proceedings relate to an indictable offence or an offence punishable on summary conviction.

(4) In proceedings under this Act, subsection 786(2) of the *Criminal Code* does not apply in respect of an indictable offence.

(5) Section 809 of the *Criminal Code* does not apply in respect of proceedings under this Act.

Counts charged in information.

53. Indictable offences and offences punishable on summary conviction may under this Act be charged in the same information and tried jointly.

Issue of subpoena — Service of subpoena.

54. (1) Where a person is required to attend to give evidence before a youth court, the subpoena directed to that person may be issued by a youth court judge, whether or not the person whose attendance is required is within the same province as the youth court.

(2) A subpoena issued by a youth court and directed to a person who is not within the same province as the youth court shall be served personally on the person to whom it is directed.

Warrant.

55. A warrant that is issued out of a youth court may be executed anywhere in Canada.

EVIDENCE

General law on admissibility of statements to apply — When statements are admissible — Exception in certain cases for oral statements — Waiver of right to consult — Statements given under duress are inadmissible — Misrepresentation of age — Parent, etc. not a person in authority.

56. (1) Subject to this section, the law relating to the admissibility of statements made by persons accused of committing offences applies in respect of young persons.

(2) No oral or written statement given by a young person to a peace officer or to any other person who is, in law, a person in authority on the arrest or detention of the young person or in circumstances where the peace officer or other person has reasonable grounds for believing that the young person has committed an offence is admissible against the young person unless

(*a*) the statement was voluntary;

(*b*) the person to whom the statement was given has, before the statement was made, clearly explained to the young person, in language appropriate to his age and understanding, that

(i) the young person is under no obligation to give a statement,

(ii) any statement given by him may be used as evidence in proceedings against him,

(iii) the young person has the right to consult counsel and a parent or other person in accordance with paragraph (*c*), and

(iv) any statement made by the young person is required to be made in the presence of counsel and any other person consulted in accordance with paragraph (*c*), if any, unless the young person desires otherwise;

(*c*) the young person has, before the statement was made, been given a reasonable opportunity to consult

(i) with counsel, and

(ii) a parent, or in the absence of a parent, an adult relative, or in the absence of a parent and an adult relative, any other appropriate adult chosen by the young person; and

(*d*) where the young person consults any person pursuant to paragraph (*c*), the young person has been given a reasonable opportunity to make the statement in the presence of that person.

(3) The requirements set out in paragraphs (2)(*b*), (*c*) and (*d*) do not apply in respect of oral statements where they are made spontaneously by the young person to a peace officer or other person in authority before that person has had a reasonable opportunity to comply with those requirements.

(4) A young person may waive the rights under paragraph (2)(*c*) or (*d*) but any such waiver shall be videotaped or be in writing, and where it is in writing it shall contain a statement signed by the young person that the young person has been apprised of the right being waived.

(5) A youth court judge may rule inadmissible in any proceedings under this Act a statement given by the young person in respect of whom the proceedings are taken if the young person satisfies the judge that the statement was given under duress imposed by any person who is not, in law, a person in authority.

(5.1) A youth court judge may in any proceedings under this Act rule admissible any statement or waiver by a young person where, at the time of the making of the statement or waiver,

(*a*) the young person held himself or herself to be eighteen years of age or older;

(*b*) the person to whom the statement or waiver was made conducted reasonable inquiries as to the age of the young person and had reasonable grounds for believing that the young person was eighteen years of age or older; and

(*c*) in all other circumstances the statement or waiver would otherwise be admissible.

(6) For the purpose of this section, an adult consulted pursuant to paragraph 56(2)(*c*) shall, in the absence of evidence to the contrary, be deemed not to be a person in authority. R.S. 1985, c. 24 (2d Supp.), s. 38; 1995, c. 19, s. 35.

Testimony of a parent — Evidence of age by certificate or record — Other evidence — When age may be inferred.

57. (1) In any proceedings under this Act, the testimony of a parent as to the age of a person of whom he is a parent is admissible as evidence of the age of that person.

(2) In any proceedings under this Act,

(*a*) a birth or baptismal certificate or a copy thereof purporting to be certified under the hand of the person in whose custody those records are held is evidence of the age of the person named in the certificate or copy; and

(*b*) an entry or record of an incorporated society that has had the control or care of the person alleged to have committed the offence in respect of which the proceedings are taken at or about the time the person came to Canada is evidence of the age of that person, if the entry or record was made before the time when the offence is alleged to have been committed.

(3) In the absence, before the youth court, of any certificate, copy, entry or record mentioned in subsection (2), or in corroboration of any such certificate, copy, entry or record, the youth court may receive and act on any other information relating to age that it considers reliable.

(4) In any proceedings under this Act, the youth court may draw inferences as to the age of a person from the person's appearance or from statements made by the person in direct examination or cross-examination.

Admissions — Other party may adduce evidence.

58. (1) A party to any proceedings under this Act may admit any relevant fact or matter for the purpose of dispensing with proof thereof, including any fact or matter the admissibility of which depends on a ruling of law or of mixed law and fact.

(2) Nothing in this section precludes a party to a proceeding from adducing evidence to prove a fact or matter admitted by another party.

Material evidence.

59. Any evidence material to proceedings under this Act that would not but for this section be admissible in evidence may, with the consent of the parties to the proceedings and where the young person is represented by counsel, be given in such proceedings.

Evidence of a child or young person.

60. In any proceedings under this Act where the evidence of a child or a young person is taken, it shall be taken only after the youth court judge or the justice, as the case may be, has

(*a*) in all cases, if the witness is a child, and

(*b*) where he deems it necessary, if the witness is a young person,

instructed the child or young person as to the duty of the witness to speak the truth and the consequences of failing to do so.

(2), (3) [Repealed R.S. 1985, c. 24 (2d Supp.), s. 39.]
R.S. 1985, c. 24 (2d Supp.), s. 39.

61. [Repealed R.S. 1985, c. 24 (2d Supp.), s. 40.]

Proof of service — Proof of signature and official character unnecessary.

62. (1) For the purposes of this Act, service of any document may be proved by oral evidence given under oath by, or by the affidavit or statutory declaration of, the person claiming to have personally served it or sent it by mail.

(2) Where proof of service of any document is offered by affidavit or statutory declaration, it is not necessary to prove the signature or official character of the person making or taking the affidavit or declaration, if the official character of that person appears on the face thereof.

Seal not required.

63. It is not necessary to the validity of any information, summons, warrant, minute, disposition, conviction, order or other process or document laid, issued, filed or entered in any proceedings under this Act that any seal be attached or affixed thereto.

SUBSTITUTION OF JUDGES

Powers of substitute youth court judge — Transcript of evidence already given

64. (1) A youth court judge who acts in the place of another youth court judge pursuant to subsection 669.2(1) of the *Criminal Code* shall,

(*a*) if an adjudication has been made, proceed with the disposition of the case or make the order that, in the circumstances, is authorized by law; or

(*b*) if no adjudication has been made, recommence the trial as if no evidence had been taken.

(2) Where a youth court judge recommences a trial under paragraph (1)(*b*), he may, if the parties consent, admit into evidence a transcript of any evidence already given in the case. R.S. 1985, c. 27 (1st Supp.), s. 187, Schedule V.

FUNCTIONS OF CLERKS OF COURTS

Powers of clerks.

65. In addition to any powers conferred on a clerk of a court by the *Criminal Code*, a clerk of the youth court may exercise such powers as are ordinarily exercised by a clerk of a court, and, in particular, may

(*a*) administer oaths or solemn affirmations in all matters relating to the business of the youth court; and

(*b*) in the absence of a youth court judge, exercise all the powers of a youth court judge relating to adjournment.

FORMS, REGULATIONS AND RULES OF COURT

Forms — Where forms not prescribed.

66. (1) The forms prescribed under section 67, varied to suit the case, or forms to the like effect, are valid and sufficient in the circumstances for which they are provided.

(2) In any case for which forms are not prescribed under section 67, the forms set out in Part XXVIII of the *Criminal Code*, with such modifications as the circumstances require, or other appropriate forms, may be used. R.S. 1985, c. 1 (4th Supp.), s. 43.

Regulations.

67. (1) The Governor in Council may make regulations

(*a*) prescribing forms that may be used for the purposes of this Act;

(*b*) establishing uniform rules of court for youth courts across Canada, including rules regulating the practice and procedure to be followed by youth courts; and

(*c*) generally for carrying out the purposes and provisions of this Act. R.S. 1985, c. 24 (2d Supp.), s. 41.

Youth court may make rules — Rules of court — Publication of rules.

68. (1) Every youth court for a province may, at any time with the concurrence of a majority of the judges thereof present at a meeting held for the purpose and subject to the approval of the Lieutenant Governor in Council, establish rules of court not inconsistent with this Act or any other Act of Parliament or with any regulations made pursuant to section 67 regulating proceedings within the jurisdiction of the youth court.

(2) Rules under subsection (1) may be made

(*a*) generally to regulate the duties of the officers of the youth court and any other matter considered expedient to attain the ends of justice and carry into effect the provisions of this Act;

(*b*) subject to any regulations made under paragraph 67(b), to regulate the practice and procedure in the youth court; and

(*c*) to prescribe forms to be used in the youth court where not otherwise provided for by or pursuant to this Act.

(3) Rules of court that are made under the authority of this section shall be published in the appropriate provincial gazette.

YOUTH JUSTICE COMMITTEES

Youth justice committees.
69. The Attorney General of a province or such other Minister as the Lieutenant Governor in Council of the province may designate, or a delegate thereof, may establish one or more committees of citizens, to be known as youth justice committees, to assist without remuneration in any aspect of the administration of this Act or in any programs or services for young offenders and may specify the method of appointment of committee members and the functions of the committees.

AGREEMENTS WITH PROVINCES

Agreements with provinces.
70. Any Minister of the Crown may, with the approval of the Governor in Council, enter into an agreement with the government of any province providing for payments by Canada to the province in respect of costs incurred by the province or a municipality for care of and services provided to young persons dealt with under this Act. R.S. 1985, c. 24 (2d Supp.), s. 42.

SCHEDULE
(Section 36)
(Subsections 45(2.1) and 45.02(3) and (4))

1. An offence under any of the following provisions of the *Criminal Code*:
    (*a*) paragraph 81(2)(*a*) (causing injury with intent);
    (*b*) section 85 (use of firearm during commission of offence);

    (*b*) subsection 85(1) (using firearm in commission of offences); 1995, c. 39, s. 189(*e*). Not in force at date of publication.

    (*c*) section 151 (sexual interference);
    (*d*) section 152 (invitation to sexual touching);
    (*e*) section 153 (sexual exploitation);
    (*f*) section 155 (incest);
    (*g*) section 159 (anal intercourse);
    (*h*) section 170 (parent or guardian procuring sexual activity by child);
    (*i*) subsection 212(2) (living off the avails of prostitution by a child);
    (*j*) subsection 212(4) (obtaining sexual services of a child);
    (*k*) section 236 (manslaughter);
    (*l*) section 239 (attempt to commit murder);
    (*m*) section 267 (assault with a weapon or causing bodily harm);
    (*n*) section 268 (aggravated assault);
    (*o*) section 269 (unlawfully causing bodily harm);
    (*p*) section 271 (sexual assault);
    (*q*) section 272 (sexual assault with a weapon, threats to a third party or causing bodily harm);
    (*r*) section 273 (aggravated sexual assault);
    (*s*) section 279 (kidnapping);
    (*t*) section 344 (robbery);
    (*u*) section 433 (arson — disregard for human life);
    (*v*) section 434.1 (arson — own property);
    (*w*) section 436 (arson by negligence); and
    (*x*) paragraph 465(1)(*a*) (conspiracy to commit murder).
2. An offence under any of the following provisions of the *Criminal Code*, as they read immediately before July 1, 1990:
    (*a*) section 433 (arson);
    (*b*) section 434 (setting fire to other substance); and
    (*c*) section 436 (setting fire by negligence).

3. An offence under any of the following provisions of the *Criminal Code*, chapter C-34 of the Revised Statutes of Canada, 1970, as they read immediately before January 4, 1983:

> (*a*) section 144 (rape);
> (*b*) section 145 (attempt to commit rape);
> (*c*) section 149 (indecent assault on female);
> (*d*) section 156 (indecent assault on male); and
> (*e*) section 246 (assault with intent).

4. An offence under any of the following provisions of the *Narcotic Control Act*:

> (*a*) section 4 (trafficking); and
> (*b*) section 5 (importing and exporting).

1995, c. 19, s. 36.

Conditional Amendment

If Bill C-7 [now Bill C-8], introduced during the first session of the thirty-fifth Parliament is assented to, then when ss. 6 and 7 come into force, item 4 of the schedule is replaced with:

4. An offence under any of the following provisions of the *Controlled Drugs and Substances Act*:

> (*a*) section 6 (trafficking); and
> (*b*) section 7 (importing and exporting).

1995, c. 19, s. 42

Appendix B
Forms and Letters

FORM 1
Notice of Motion for Adjournment (Defense Counsel)

IN THE ONTARIO COURT (PROVINCIAL DIVISION)

BETWEEN:

HER MAJESTY THE QUEEN

Respondent

and

YOUR CLIENT

Applicant

NOTICE OF MOTION FOR ADJOURNMENT

Please take note that on Thursday,   1993, at 2:00 p.m. or so soon thereafter as the motion can be heard, the Applicant will make a motion to H_____ Honour Judge   for an adjournment of a disposition hearing which is scheduled to take place Tuesday, July 13 at   a.m. The motion will be heard in Youth Court, 311 Jarvis St., Toronto, Ontario.

The grounds for this motion are that counsel for the young person is now required to attend   on July 13, 1993. The applicant will rely on further particulars which will be submitted at the time of this motion.

Dated this   day of   , 1993.

John Hook
Barrister and Solicitor
210 Queen Street East, Suite 1101
Toronto, Ontario
(416) 922-1680

TO: The Clerk of the Ontario Court (Provincial Division)
       311 Jarvis Street
       Toronto, Ontario

AND TO: The Crown Attorney
           Ontario Court (Provincial Division)
           311 Jarvis Street
           Toronto, Ontario

FORM 2
Notice of Motion for Adjournment (Crown Counsel)

ONTARIO COURT (PROVINCIAL DIVISION)
COUR DE L'ONTARIO (DIVISION PROVINCIALE)

TORONTO REGION
RÉGION DE TORONTO

REGINA vs. ....
SA MAJESTE LA REINE C

CHARGE ....ASSAULT........ SLC .... 266 .... C.C.C. ....
ACCUSATION

A matter set for hearing ....Thursday.... the .... day of ......July...... , 19.....
Affaire inscrite au rôle pour le   *jour de*

in Courtroom No. ....300...... at .... 1000 Finch Ave. W. ....
en salle d'audience n°   *à*

NOTICE OF APPLICATION FOR ADJOURNMENT
AVIS DE REQUÉTE EN ADJOURNEMENT

Take notice that the ....Crown........ will apply on ......Tuesday......
Sachez que   *demandera, le*

the ....3rd.... day of May   1994

                                    to the presiding Judge in Courtroom
jour de   *au juge qui siègera en la salle d'audience*

No. ....300..... at .....0930.....o'clock in the .....fore..... noon or so soon thereafter
n°   *à*   *heures   au aussitôt après, des que la requête*
as the application can be heard for an adjournment of the above matter on the grounds that:
pourra être entendue, d'accorder l'ajournement de l'affaire susmentionnée pour les motifs suivants:

....
..............Witness will be ....
...............out of country, month of ....
............July 1994..

DATED at the Municipality of Metropolitan Toronto, in the Toronto Region,
FAIT dans la municipalité de la communauté urbaine de Toronto, dans la région de Toronto,

this ....27th........ day of ....April.......... , 1994
ce   *jour de*

156

FORM 2 — continued

	Counsel for	
....	*avocat pour*	....
....	Counsel for	....
	avocat pour	
....	Counsel for	....
	avocat pour	

FORM 3
Notice of Motion under Section 8 of the Young Offenders Act

ONTARIO COURT (PROVINCIAL DIVISION)

BETWEEN:

HER MAJESTY THE QUEEN

Respondent

and

YOUR CLIENT

Applicant

NOTICE OF MOTION

TAKE NOTICE that an application will be made by Counsel on behalf of the Applicant, before the presiding Justice at 311 Jarvis Street, Toronto, Ontario on Monday September 20, 1993 at 10:00 o'clock in the forenoon or so soon thereafter as the application may be heard for an Order pursuant to Section 8 of the Young Offenders Act vacating the Order previously made by a Justice of the Peace on Wednesday September 22, 1993, 311 Jarvis Street, Toronto, Ontario, ordering that the Applicant, be released from custody pursuant to Section 8 of the Young Offenders Act.

DATE: September 22, 1993.

JOHN HOOK
Barrister & Solicitor
210 Queen Street East
Toronto,Ontario
M4M 1H7

(416) 922-1680

Charge: Assault Bodily Harm

Counsel for the Applicant

FORM 4
Consent to the Disclosure, Transmittal or Examination of a Clincial Record

Form 14	**Consent to the Disclosure, Transmittal**
Mental Health Act	**or Examination of a Clinical Record**

I, _____
(print full name of person)

of _____
(address)

hereby consent to the disclosure or transmittal to or the examination by

_____
(print name)

of the clinical record compiled in _____
(name of psychiatric facility)

in respect of _____
(name of patient)

See
Note 5.

_____
(signature)

_____
(witness)

Dated the _____ day of _____ 19 _____

Notes:

1. Consent to the disclosure, transmittal or examination of a clinical record may be given by the patient or (where the patient has not attained the age of majority or is not mentally competent) by the nearest relative of the patient.

   See subsection 29(3) of the Act.

2. Patient.

   Clause 29(1)(b) of the Act states that "'patient' includes former patient, out-patient and former out-patient".

3. Mentally competent.

   Clause 1(h) of the Act defines "mentally competent" as "having the ability to understand the subject-matter in respect of which consent is requested and able to appreciate the consequences of giving or withholding consent".

4. Nearest relative.

   Clause 1(j) of the Act is as follows:

   " 'nearest relative' means,

   (i) The spouse who is of any age and men-

   tally competent, or

   (ii) if none or if the spouse is not available, any one of the children who has attained the age of majority and is mentally competent, or

   (iii) if none or if none is available, either of the parents who is mentally competent or the guardian, or

   (iv) if none or if neither is available, any one of the brothers or sisters who has attained the age of majority and is mentally competent, or

   (v) if none or if none is available, any other of the next of kin who has attained the age of majority and is mentally competent".

5. Signature.

   Where the consent is signed by the nearest relative, the relationship to the patient must be set out below the signature of the nearest relative.

   O. Reg. 609/80 s. 16(14)

FORM 5
Request for Alternative Measures

YOUTH COURT
CANADA
PROVINCE OF ONTARIO

ALTERNATIVE MEASURES
(Section 4, the Young Offenders Act)

PART I

....
(Region)

REQUEST FOR ALTERNATIVE MEASURES

Youth's name ....
.... Last .... First .... Middle

Address: ....

Postal Code: .... Date of Birth: .... Telephone No ....

I hereby request that I be considered for a program of alternative measures in relation to the following offence(s)

(1)

(2)

I acknowledge that:
(1) I have been advised of my right to be represented by counsel;
(2) I have been given a reasonable opportunity to consult with counsel;
(3) I accept responsibility for the acts or omissions as attached in the copy of the enclosed synopsis that form the basis of the offence(s) stated above in respect of which I request alternative measures;
(4) I have been informed of the alternative measures available;
(5) I fully and freely consent to participate in those alternative measures.

I acknowledge that:
(1) I have not been found guilty of any criminal offence(s). (if yes, give details)

(2) I was not part of an Alternative Measures program in the past. (if yes, give details)

(3) I have no other criminal charges outstanding against me. (if yes, give details)

_____   _____
Signature of Youth   Signature of Witness

....
Date   Date Served on Crown's Office

_____   Court: ....
Next Court Appearance Date

Officer-in-Charge: ....   Police Division: ....

Synopsis of offence must be attached. Please leave with secretary at Crown's office.

PART II
Acknowledgement and Recommendation by Agent of the Attorney General

Based on the Crown Brief prepared at today's date:
(1) In my opinion, sufficient evidence exists to proceed with the prosecution of each of the offences in respect of which this request for alternative measures is made.
(2) The prosecution of the offence(s) in respect of which this request for the alternative measures is made appears not to be barred in law
(3) I am satisfied (not satisfied), having regard to the interests of society, that it may be appropriate to use alternative measures in relation to the offence(s) referred to in this request
(4) I recommend (do not recommend) that the Provincial Director inquire into the needs of the young person and determine the suitability of the youth referred to herein for alternative measures.

_____   _____
Date   Agent of the Attorney General

PART III
Acknowledgement by Provincial Director

(1) I am satisfied (not satisfied) that having regard to the needs of the young person, it would be appropriate to use alternative measures in relation to the offence(s) referred to in this request
(2) I am satisfied (not satisfied) that the young person is a suitable candidate for admission to the alternative measures program
(3) The young person has agreed to perform the following alternative measures:

(4) The anticipated time period for completion of these measures is:

_____   _____
Date   Provincial Director or Agent

160

FORM 6
Notice of Motion for Production

ONTARIO COURT OF JUSTICE
(PROVINCIAL DIVISION)
YOUTH COURT

BETWEEN:

HER MAJESTY THE QUEEN

and

YOUR CLIENT

NOTICE OF MOTION

TAKE NOTICE that the accused,   , will make
a motion before His Honour Judge   on
at 9:30 a.m., or as soon after that time as the motion can be heard, at the Provincial
Court House, 1911 Eglinton Avenue East, Scarborough, Ontario in Youth Court
(#408 or Family Court #2).

The motion is for:
1. An order for production to counsel for the defence of the Ontario School Record
and any other behavioural record, note, document or letter concerning the witness
          . Pursuant to a subpoena dated March 8, 1994 and served March 8,
1994, these documents will be returned to the Court on the date of the motion by
the records keeper of   , Scarborough Board of Education.

The grounds for this motion are:
1. Section 266 of the *Education Act*, R.S.O. 1990, C.E.2, which purports to attach
privilege to the subpoena-ed documents, is either *ultra vires* or inoperative in a
criminal matter being heard pursuant to the *Young Offenders Act*, by virtue of the
decision of the Supreme Court of Canada in *Marshall v. R.* (1960), 129 C.C.C. 232,
and by virtue of the *Canadian Charter of Rights and Freedoms*, section 7.

2. In order to properly prepare cross-examination, the defence requires this material
for a period of time prior to the trial. The trial date is now set for April 14, 1994.

3. Such further and other grounds as counsel may advise and this honourable Court
permit.

Dated at Toronto this 6th day of April, 1994.

JOHN HOOK
Barrister and Solicitor
210 Queen Street East, Suite 1101
Toronto, Ontario

(416) 922-1680
Of counsel for the accused,

To:

The Clerk of this Honourable Court

And to:

Crown Attorney
Ontario Court (Provincial Division)
1911 Eglinton Avenue East
Scarborough, Ontario

FORM 7
Notice of Review of Disposition

<table>
<tr><td>

YOUTH COURT
TRIBUNAL DE LA JEUNESSE
CANADA
PROVINCE OF ONTARIO
PROVINCE DE L'ONTARIO
YORK
(County/comté, district etc.)

</td><td>

NOTICE OF REVIEW OF DISPOSITION
AVIS EN MATIÈRE D'EXAMEN
(Sections 28 to 32, The Young Offenders Act)
(Articles 28 à 32, Loi sur les jeunes contrevenants)

</td></tr>
</table>

To/À
(1) (Name of Parent)
(2) CROWN ATTORNEY'S OFFICE, 311 JARVIS STREET, TORONTO ONTARIO
(3) (Name), SPRUCEDALE YOUTH CENTRE, P.O. BOX 606, SIMCOE, ONTARIO
(4) (Name), SPRUCEDALE YOUTH CENTRE, P.O. BOX 606, SIMCOE, ONTARIO

(1) being a parent, within the meaning of the Young Offenders Act, of the hereinafter named youth;

en votre qualité de père ou de mère, au sens de ce terme dans la Loi sur les jeunes contrevenants, de l'adolescent nommé ci-dessous;

(2) being the Attorney General;
en votre qualité de procureur général.

(3) being an agent of the Attorney General
en votre qualité de représentant du procureur général.

(4) being the provincial director
en votre qualité de directeur provincial.

WHEREAS on the 28 day of OCTOBER 1993,
ATTENDU QUE le

a young person within the meaning of the Young Offenders Act, was found guilty of the following offence(s)
adolescent au sens de ce terme dans la Loi sur les jeunes contrevenants, a été déclaré(e) coupable de l'infraction suivante (ou des infractions suivantes): (State offence(s)/préciser (les) l'infraction(s))

ROBBERY X2
WEAPONS DANGEROUS

AND WHEREAS, by order of disposition dated the 28 day of OCTOBER 1993, it was ordered that:
ATTENDU QUE, par ordonnance portant décision en date du , il a été ordonné que
(State disposition as contained in order/indiquer la disposition telle que contenue dans l'ordonnance)

8 MONTHS SECURE CUSTODY
18 MONTHS PROBATION

AND WHEREAS ☐ a review of the disposition is required pursuant to subsection 28(1) of the Young Offenders Act;
ATTENDU QUE conformément au paragraphe 28(1) de la Loi sur les jeunes contrevenants, il doit être procédé à l'examen de la décision;

☒ an application has been made by .... for a review of the disposition;
une demande d'examen a été présentée par

THIS IS THEREFORE TO NOTIFY YOU that the review will be heard before the Youth Court
À CES CAUSES, LES PRÉSENTES ONT POUR OBJET DE VOUS AVISER QUE procédera à l'examen de la décision à

at 311 JARVIS STREET, TORONTO, ONTARIO

on THURSDAY the 16 day of DECEMBER 1994, at 10:00 o'clock in the (or) noon.
le à heure(s).

AND THIS IS NOTIFY YOU that the said young person has the right to be represented by counsel;
AND THIS IS ALSO TO NOTIFY YOU that you or any person who is a parent, within the meaning of the Young Offenders Act, of the said young person may appear at the hearing and will be given an opportunity to be heard

LES PRÉSENTES ONT AUSSI POUR OBJET DE VOUS AVISER que l'adolescent a le droit d'être représenté(e) par un avocat;
LES PRÉSENTES ONT EN OUTRE POUR OBJET DE VOUS AVISER que vous ou toute autre personne, père ou mère au sens de ce terme dans la Loi sur les jeunes contrevenants de dit jeune pouvez vous présenter à l'audition et vous aurez l'occasion de présenter vos observations.

DATED this ..... day of .... ,19... , at the .... of ....
FAIT le , à le de

in the Province of Ontario.
dans la province de l'Ontario.

_____
A Judge of the Youth Court
Juge de tribunal de la jeunesse

FORM 7 — *continued*

AFFIDAVIT OF SERVICE

CANADA
PROVINCE OF ONTARIO

I, ...
of the .... of .... , make oath and say that
I did on .... day, the .... day of .... ,19 .
serve
with a true copy of the within notice in the manner indicated below: namely.

*Place
mark in
appropriate
box

(a) by delivering it to him/her personally.
(b) by mailing it by ordinary/registered mail to ....
at ....
his last know or usual place of abode.

I, ...
of the .... of .... , make oath and say that
I did on .... day, the .... day of .... ,19 .
serve ....
with a true copy of the within notice in the manner indicated below: namely,

*Place
mark in
appropriate
box

(a) by delivering it to him/her personally.
(b) by mailing it by ordinary/registered mail to ....
at ....
his last know or usual place of abode.

I, ...
of the .... of .... , make oath and say that
I did on .... day, the .... day of .... ,19 .
serve ....
with a true copy of the within notice in the manner indicated below: namely.

*Place
mark in
appropriate
box

(a) by delivering it to him/her personally.
(b) by mailing it by ordinary/registered mail to ....
at ....
his last know or usual place of abode.

Sworn before me at ....   _____
....   *Signature*
this .... day of .... , 19   No. .... Div. ....
....

A Justice of the Peace in and for the Province of Ontario
or the County/District of

FORM 8
Notice to Young Person of Review of Disposition

NOTICE TO YOUNG PERSON OF REVIEW OF DISPOSITION
AVIS À L'ADOLESCENT EN MATIÈRE D'EXAMEN D'UNE DÉCISION

YOUTH COURT
TRIBUNAL DE LA JEUNESSE
CANADA
PROVINCE OF ONTARIO
PROVINCE DE L'ONTARIO
YORK
(Region/Région)

(Sections 28 to 32, The Young Offenders Act)

(Article 28 à 32, Loi sur les jeunes contrevenants)

To /À .... of/de .... CITY OF TORONTO ....

a young person within the meaning of the Young Offenders Act,
adolescent(e) au sens de ce terme dans la Loi sur les jeunes contrevenants,

WHEREAS, on the .. 28 . day of .. OCTOBER 19 .. 93 .. you were found guilty of the following offence(s) (state offences)
ATTENDU QUE le ...., vous avez été déclaré(e) coupable de l'infraction suivante (ou des infractions

suivantes) (préciser (les) l'infraction(s))

ROBBERY X2
WEAPONS DANGEROUS

AND WHEREAS, by order of disposition dated the .. 28 . day of .... OCTOBER .... 19 . 93 , it was ordered that
ATTENDU QUE, par ordonnance portant décision en date du ...., il a été ordonné que
(state disposition as contained in order/indiquer la disposition contenue dans l'ordonnance)

8 MONTHS SECURE CUSTODY
18 MONTHS PROBATION

AND WHEREAS ☐ a review of the disposition is required pursuant to subsection 28(1) of the Young Offenders Act,
ATTENDU QUE   *conformément au paragraphe 28(1) de la Loi sur les jeunes contrevenants, il doit être procédé à*
l'examen de la décision,

   ☒ an application has been made by ....
une demande d'examen de la décision a été présentée par

for a review of the disposition;

THIS IS THEREFORE TO NOTIFY YOU that the review will be heard before the Youth Court at
À CES CAUSES, LES PRÉSENTES ONT POUR OBJET DE VOUS AVISER que le tribunal procédera à l'examen de la décision
at .. 311 JARVIS STREET, TORONTO, ONTARIO ....
à

on .. THURSDAY .., the .. 16 day of .. December .... 19 . 94 , at .... 10:00 .. o'clock in the .. fore .. noon
le .... à .... heure(s)

AND this is to notify you that you have the right to be represented by counsel
LES PRÉSENTES ont aussi pour objet de vous aviser que vous avez le droit de vous faire représenter par un avocat

DATED this .... day of .... 19.... at the .... of ....
FAIT le .... , à la .... de

in the Province of Ontario.
dans la province de l'Ontario.

_____
A Judge of the Youth Court
Juge du tribunal de la jeunesse

YO 011 (rev 03/90)

164

FORM 9
Letter Requiring Destruction of Records

Dear Sir/Madam:

Re: Young Person Smith
DOB: August 15, 1980
Charges: Break & Enter with intent

This letter confirms that on January 15, 1994, Mr. Smith appeared in Courtroom #7, 311 Jarvis Street, Toronto, before Her Honour Judge Hatton for trial. He was found not guilty on the charge.

My client's fingerprints and photographs were taken pursuant to the *Identification of Criminals Act.*

In the light of the fact that this charge did not result in a finding of guilt, and it is now two months after the period for appeal has expired, I would ask that you either return my client's fingerprints and photographs to me as his solicitor or confirm with me that they have been destroyed.

Yours truly,

FORM 10
Notice of Application For "Transfer Down" Hearing
(Defence Counsel)

Court File No.

ONTARIO COURT
(PROVINCIAL DIVISION)
Youth Court

B E T W E E N:

HER MAJESTY THE QUEEN

Respondent

and

Applicant

NOTICE OF APPLICATION

TAKE NOTICE THAT an application will be brought on   day of
            , 1996 at [specify date and location] for an order pursuant to section 16(1.01) of the *Young Offenders Act* that the charges against the applicant be proceeded with in youth court.

THE GROUNDS FOR THE APPLICATION ARE:

1. That given the circumstances of the alleged offences, the age, maturity, character and background of the applicant, the availability of resources in the youth system and the adequacy of the YOA to deal with the applicant, the objectives referred to in section 16(1.1) of the *Act* can be reconciled by the applicant being under the jurisdiction of the youth court.

8. Such further and other grounds as counsel may advise and this Honourable Court may permit.

IN SUPPORT OF THIS APPLICATION, THE APPLICANT RELIES UPON THE FOLLOWING:

1. The Pre-disposition Report dated _____;

2. The Report of the Child Advocate's Office, dated _____;

3. The Assessment of Dr. xyz, dated _____;

4. The vive voce evidence of the applicant; and

5. The vive voce evidence of the applicant's parents.

6. Such other evidence as the applicant may submit.

FORM 10 — continued

THE RELIEF SOUGHT IS FOR:

1. An Order that the charges of murder (give details relating to the informations) against the applicant be proceeded against in youth court.

THE APPLICANT MAY BE SERVED WITH THE DOCUMENTS PERTINENT TO THIS APPLICATION.

1. By service at: address etc.

Dated at Toronto, this   day of   ,1996.

_____
(Name and address of counsel)

TO: Crown Attorney
    Clerk of the Court
    Parents of the young person

FORM 11
Notice of Constitutional Question (Defence Counsel)

IN THE MATTER of the review of disposition of xyz., a young person, pursuant to section 28 of the *Young Offenders Act* R.S.C., 1985, c. Y-1, as amended

B E T W E E N:

xyz. (a young person)

Applicant

- and -

Her Majesty The Queen

Respondent

NOTICE OF CONSTITUTIONAL QUESTION

1. The Applicant intends to seek relief pursuant to section 24 (1) of the *Canadian Charter of Rights and Freedoms* in the context of the review of his disposition, relating to his treatment at yyy detention centre on　　　　at a hearing before the Youth Court on Friday June 28th, 1996 at　　　　courtroom #1 at 9:30 a.m. or at such other time as the matter can be heard.

2. The following are the material facts giving rise to the Constitutional question:

    (1) The Applicant was born _____ .

    (2) The Applicant is serving the following disposition: _____ .

    (3) The Applicant was subjected to _____ .

3. The following is the legal basis for the Constitutional Question:

    (1) The applicant relies on section 12 of the *Charter* which provides that:

    Everyone has the right not to be subjected to any cruel and unusual treatment or punishment.

    And further, on section 7 of the *Charter* which provides that:

    (7) Everyone has the right to life, liberty and security of the person and the right not to be deprived thereof except in accordance with the principles of fundamental justice.

4. The applicant seeks the following relief pursuant to section 24(1) of the *Charter*:

    1. A stay of the remainder of his disposition.

In the alternative, pursuant to section 28 of the *Act* and section 24(1) of the *Charter*:

    2. An order that he be placed on probation for the remainder of his disposition; or,

FORM 11 — continued

3. An order that he be placed in open custody for the remainder of his disposition, subject to any early release provisions or orders.

4. Such other relief as this Honourable Court may deem just.

Dated at   the   day of   , 1   .

_____

Counsel for the Applicant

TO: Crown Attorney
    Attorney General of (Province)
    Federal Attorney General
    Clerk of the Court

FORM 12
Judge's Order Requiring Transportation of Young Person To Court From Custody
Facility (Defence Counsel)

ONTARIO COURT (PROVINCIAL DIVISION)

THE HONOURABLE	) FRIDAY THE 17TH DAY OF
JUDGE	) JANUARY, 1997
	)

B E T W E E N:

REGINA

Respondent

and

GW.

Applicant

ORDER

TO THE OFFICERS of the Sprucedale Youth Centre, Simcoe, Ontario and to all Peace Officers in Ontario.

WHEREAS the attendance of the Applicant, GW, is required for a court appearance on three outstanding charges, and whereas he is in custody at the above noted youth centre and his attendance is material to the proceedings.

1. THIS COURT ORDERS that the Applicant, GW, be brought before this court on Thursday the 22nd day of January, 1997 at 10:00 o'clock in the forenoon to Ontario Court (Provincial Division)   , Ontario, and that he be returned and readmitted immediately thereafter to the above Youth Centre unless the Court should otherwise direct.

_____
THE HONOURABLE JUDGE

TO: THE CLERK OF THIS HONOURABLE COURT

FORM 13
Affidavit In Support of Judge's Order
(Defence Counsel)

ONTARIO COURT (PROVINCIAL DIVISION)

BE T W E E N:

REGINA

Respondent

and

GW

Applicant

AFFIDAVIT FOR JUDGE'S ORDER

I, Counsel, of the City of Toronto, in the Judicial District of York, make oath and say that:

1. I am the lawyer representing the above accused, and as such have knowledge of the matters hereinafter deposed to.

2. GW has an outstanding warrant in   on charges of theft over $5,000.00 and two breaches of probation.   of the Crown Attorney's Office and I have discussed the case and agreed that GW (the applicant) should turn himself in and speak to these matters on January 22nd, 1997 at 10:00 a.m. in Ontario Court (Provincial Division),   Ontario. GW's attendance is required and GW is presently in custody at Sprucedale Youth Centre, Simcoe, Ontario.

3. I make this affidavit for the purpose of obtaining a Judge's Order and for no other purpose.

SWORN before me this 16th day of
January, 1997 in the city of Toronto,
in the Municipality of Metropolitan
Toronto.

_____	)))	_____
A Commissioner, etc.		Counsel

Appendix C
Bibliography of Relevant Social Science Literature

- Peterson, *Children's Understanding of the Juvenile Justice System: A Cognitive-Developmental Perspective*, Cdn. J. of Criminology, Oct. 1988 p. 381.

- Peterson-Badali and Abramovitch, *Children's Knowledge of the Legal System: Are They Competent to Instruct Legal Counsel?*, Cdn. J. of Criminology, April 1992 p. 139.

- Peterson-Badali and Abramovitch, *Grade Related Changes in Young Person's Reasoning About Plea Decision*, Law and Human Behaviour (in press).

- Read, *Minors' Ability to Participate in the Adjudication Process: A Look at Their Understanding of Court Proceedings and Legal Rights*, M.A. Dissertation, Centre of Criminology, University of Toronto, September 1987.

- Abramovitch, and Peterson-Badali, *Young Persons' Comprehension of Waivers and Statements*, Canadian Bar Association, Ontario Continuing Legal Education Publications, November 14, 1992.

Appendix D
List of Child Advocates Across Canada

Joyce Preston
Child, Youth and Family Advocate
Suite 2050
200 Granville Street
VANCOUVER BC V6C 1S4
Tel: (604) 775-3149
Fax: (604) 775 3205
Email:JPRESTON@Galaxy.gov.bc.ca

Penny Parry
Child and Youth Advocate
Social Planning Department
250 West Heritage Building
City Square, Box 96
555 West 12th Avenue
VANCOUVER BC V5Z 3X7
Tel: (604) 871-6032
Fax: (604) 871-6048
Email:PennyParry@mindlink.bc.ca

John LaFrance
Children's Advocate
10109 - 106th Street
EDMONTON AB T5J 3L7
Tel: (403) 427-8934
Email:jlafrand@tibalt.supernet.ab.ca

Wayne Govereau
Children's Advocate
503 - 330 Graham Avenue
WINNIPEG MB R3C 4A5
Tel: (204) 945-1427
      1-800-263-7146
Fax: (204) 948-2278

Judy Finlay, Manager
Office of Child and Family Services
Advocacy
Program Management Division
Ministry of Community and Social
Services
10th Floor, 2195 Yonge Street
TORONTO ON M7A 1G2
Tel: (416) 325-5989
     (416) 325-5669
     1-800-263-2841
Fax: (416) 325-5681
Secretary: Angela

Celine Giroux
Commission des droits de la personne
et de la jeunesse du Quebec
360, rue Saint-Jacques
MONTREAL QC H2Y 1P5
Tel: (514) 873-5146
     1-800-361-6477
Fax: (514) 873-2373

Richard Abraham
Researcher/Analyst
P.O. Box 8700
ST. JOHN'S NF A1B 4J6
Tel: (709) 729-2683
Fax: (709) 729-4820

Index

Canada Practice Guides
C R I M I N A L S E R I E S

ORDER FORM — PLEASE TEAR ALONG EDGE TO REMOVE ORDER FORM

❑ ___copy(ies) of Appearing in Provincial Offence Court
ORDER # 954845X-819 1996 120 pp. $48 0-459-54845-X

❑ ___copy(ies) of Bail Hearings 1996
ORDER # 955400X-819 1995 160 pp. $40 0-459-55400-X

❑ ___copy(ies) of Defending Drinking and Driving Cases 1997
ORDER # 9555014-819 1997 $38 0-459-55501-4

❑ ___copy(ies) of Defending Drug Cases
ORDER # 9552945-819 1995 154 pp. $42 0-459-55294-5

❑ ___copy(ies) of Defending Mentally Disordered Persons
ORDER # 9552961-819 1995 153 pp. $35 0-459-55296-1

❑ ___copy(ies) of Defending Provincial Offence Cases in Ontario
ORDER # 9553321-819 1995 146 pp. $40 0-459-55332-1

❑ ___copy(ies) of Defending Sexual Offence Cases
ORDER # 9552325-819 1993 114 pp. $35 0-459-55232-5

❑ ___copy(ies) of Defending Young Offender Cases 1997
ORDER # 955512X-819 1997 192 pp. $38 0-459-55512-X

❑ ___copy(ies) of Indictable Appeals in Alberta
ORDER # 9547763-819 1995 130 pp. $42 0-459-54776-3

❑ ___copy(ies) of Indictable Appeals in British Columbia
ORDER # 9547569-819 1995 138 pp. $48 0-459-54756-9

❑ ___copy(ies) of Indictable Appeals in Ontario
ORDER # 9552295-819 1994 120 pp. $35 0-459-55229-5

❑ ___copy(ies) of Summary Conviction Appeals
ORDER # 9552309-819 1994 156 pp. $35 0-459-55230-9

❑ ___copy(ies) of Summary Conviction Appeals in Alberta
ORDER # 9549170-819 1997 125 pp. $48 0-459-54917-0

❑ ___copy(ies) of Summary Conviction Appeals in British Columbia
ORDER # 9555030-819 1997 120 pp. $48 0-459-55503-0

❑ Please place me on standing order for any new publications.
❑ Please place me on standing order for any new editions.
❑ Please advise me of each new publication/edition.

ALL PUBLICATIONS ARE AVAILABLE FOR A 30-DAY RISK-FREE EXAMINATION

Name

Firm

Address

City   Prov.   Postal Code

Telephone #   Fax #

❑ Payment enclosed ❑ Bill me ❑ Bill my firm ❑ Bill my Carswell acct. #   P.O.#

Charge my ❑ Visa ❑ MasterCard ❑ AMEX Card #   Expirty date   /

Signature

(ORDERS MUST INCLUDE SIGNATURE AND TELEPHONE NUMBER TO BE PROCESSED)
Shipping and handling are extra. Prices subject to change without notice and subject to applicable taxes.

03/97

3 EASY WAYS TO ORDER

PLEASE QUOTE ORDER NUMBER(S)

CALL TOLL-FREE:
1-800-387-5164

IN TORONTO
(416) 609-3800

BY FAX:
(416) 298-5082

E-MAIL:

orders@carswell.com

YOUR SATISFACTION GUARANTEE

Your satisfaction with Carswell products is guaranteed. If you are not completely satisfied with any Carswell product, simply return it within 30 days of receipt, along with the invoice marked "cancelled".

CARSWELL
Thomson Professional Publishing

One Corporate Plaza,
2075 Kennedy Road, Scarborough,
Ontario M1T 3V4
http://www.carswell.com